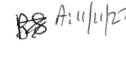

THE
UNSEEN
BRITANNIC

THE UNSEEN BRITANNIC

THE SHIP IN RARE ILLUSTRATIONS

SIMON MILLS

For Georgia

Every effort has been made by the author to seek out and acknowledge copyright ownership of all images.
If any omission has been made please contact the author via the publishers.

First published 2014
The History Press
The Mill, Brimscombe Port
Stroud, Gloucestershire, GL5 2QG
www.thehistorypress.co.uk

© Simon Mills, 2014

The right of Simon Mills to be identified as the Author of this work has been
asserted in accordance with the Copyright, Designs and Patents Act 1988.

British Library Cataloguing in Publication Data.
A catalogue record for this book is available from the British Library.

ISBN 978 0 7524 9771 6

Typesetting and origination by The History Press
Design by Katie Beard
Printed in India

CONTENTS

ACKNOWLEDGEMENTS

In a project spanning two millennia the number of people with whom I have come into contact while working on *Britannic* is impossible to list, but in that time the help and co-operation of the following has been invaluable:

Dr Robert Ballard for his visit to the wreck in 1995; Dr Evangelos Papathanassiou and Nikoleta Bellou of the Hellenic Centre for Marine Research (Elkethe) for organising the first biological survey of the wreck in 2008; Dr Roy Cullimore and Lori Johnson of Droycon Bioconcepts for their scientific analyses in 2003 and 2009, with additional historical discussions and analysis from David Hutchings, Paul Louden-Brown, Ken Marschall, Tom McCluskie, Michail Michailakis and Parks Stephenson. Also, I mustn't forget to mention Eric Sauder, who persuaded me to write this book in the first place, and Chrissy McMorris at The History Press for helping to make the process so straightforward.

Special thanks are also due to the divers of all seven *Britannic* expeditions between 1997 and 2009 who are just too numerous to list, but the team leaders include Kevin Gurr, Nick Hope, Jarrod Jablonski, John Chatterton and Richie Kohler, and the photographers include Rudi Asseer, Leigh Bishop, Antonello Paone and Kostas Katsaros, with the 2003 sonar imagery by Bill Smith and his team. I am also grateful for the co-operation of the office of the Mayor of Kea and the Greek Department of Marine Antiquities. Also deserving mention is Kirk Wolfinger of the Lone Wolf Media Company in Portland, Maine, and now a veteran of three *Britannic* expeditions in 1995, 2006 and 2009.

Closer to home, this section would not be complete without acknowledging the on-going correspondence with Harland & Wolff, and the several decades of support and co-operation that I have received from Tom McCluskie, Lorraine Goodman and Deborah Lindsay, formerly of the Technical Services Department, and more recently David McVeigh. Similarly, Captain Peter Starling of the Army Medical Services Museum (Keogh Barracks, Aldershot) has been invaluable in helping to fill in some of the gaps in regard to the medical officers who served on *Britannic*. Nor should I forget to mention the support of the former Britannic Foundation (TBF) and the Titanic Historical Society, and the friendship and support of the many relatives and descendants of *Britannic*'s crew, including Janet Baillie, Jennifer Clarke, Alasdair Fairbairn, John Fleming, Ronald Goodman, John Harvey, Margaret and Mary Meehan, Angus Mitchell, Tim and Marion Sargent and Alan Sharpe, who over the years have all patiently and generously allowed me to raid their collective memories and photographic archives.

Finally, special mention must be made of Carl Spencer, who led the dive team on the 2003 expedition to *Britannic* and helped to instigate much of the scientific work that has been achieved to date. Carl was tragically killed on 24 May 2009 while returning to the surface after a dive on the wreck – a sad reminder that sometimes the price we pay in the pursuit of knowledge really is too high.

INTRODUCTION

Why after all this time is there still this perception that *Britannic* is forgotten?

I suppose it depends on the yardstick that you use to measure the term 'forgotten'. As far as the media is concerned, *Britannic* may indeed be forgotten when compared to other ships such as *Titanic* or *Lusitania* – although eight expeditions and television documentaries on the ship would suggest otherwise – but by regarding the two earlier ships as the norm I think many researchers are just kidding themselves. While both *Titanic* and *Lusitania* were undeniably fine vessels for their time, the key issue, I believe, is that they are not remembered so much for the engineering excellence that went into their construction, but rather as leading characters in historical events over which they had no control. It was *Titanic*'s collision with the iceberg and *Lusitania*'s fate at the hands of a German torpedo that made them famous; fortunately these events were by no means the norm – and thank God for that!

Britannic is also different because she was very much not the norm. True, she was *Titanic*'s sister ship, but seeing *Britannic* in her own unique context we find a vessel that never served in the capacity for which she was designed, yet as a serving hospital ship in one of the most destructive wars ever she played an important supporting role in some of the most significant Allied campaigns during the First World War.

Finding information on *Titanic* has never been particularly difficult. Even when starting from scratch the average researcher, with reference to countless newspaper articles and two official government reports, has been provided with impressively detailed resources from which they could begin their project. The British inquiry not only published the full transcripts of the hearing, but Senator Smith's report even published the names and address of the survivors; in an era when data protection was not such an issue, I am sure that if they had e-mail addresses then Smith would have circulated them.

Your average *Britannic* researcher, however, has none of these resources to go on. Newspaper reports at the time of *Britannic*'s loss were shrouded in wartime secrecy or propaganda, and even the information that was available was scattered in official government records which, at a time when public access was not even a consideration, was effectively embargoed until the late 1960s. Even then the paperwork revealed little, with a basic report into the loss of *Britannic* amounting to barely 700 words, and compiled after a single day of interviewing a handful of the survivors scattered around Athens. The names of the thirty dead were all but lost in the mists of time, and, in that the first real book on *Britannic* was not published until more than three-quarters of a century after her loss, it is amazing that we now know so much about the ship today.

So is *Britannic* really forgotten? Never! Mysterious? Definitely. Overshadowed? Well, yes, but HMHS *Britannic* has always had her own story to tell and that story has always been as full of detail and drama as that of any of the other great vessels of the time.

Moreover, this is not just the story of a ship's past but, in this case, also of her potential future. *Titanic* lies 2½ miles down at the bottom of the Atlantic; it is cold, dark and accessible to a chosen few, with the financial and technological backing that can make the journey worthwhile. *Britannic*, on the other hand, lies barely 400ft from the surface, the crystal-clear blue waters of the Aegean Sea having all but turned the ship into a spectacular man-made coral reef, with a unique ecosystem which today supports far more life than she ever did when in service. *Titanic*'s hull is twisted and broken while *Britannic* lies as if sleeping on her starboard side, still in one magnificent piece and providing a uniquely accessible site for controlled archaeological and co-ordinated scientific study.

Britannic's future is another story. This particular narrative is all about her past, which begins ...

1
GENESIS

A postcard of *Britannic* as she would have appeared in her White Star colours. (Angus Mitchell)

At 10 a.m. on the morning of 21 June 1911, the White Star Line's brand-new steamer RMS *Olympic* had just docked at Pier 59 in New York.

With an overall length of over 882ft and at 45,324 gross tons, *Olympic* was ushering in a new age of transatlantic travel and Joseph Bruce Ismay, chairman of the White Star Line and president of the International Mercantile Marine (IMM), had every reason to feel proud of his company's latest technological triumph.

Four years earlier it had all been so different, with Cunard's *Lusitania* and *Mauretania* taking the plaudits as both the largest and fastest passenger ships in the world. The White Star reputation for comfort and reliability was under immense pressure and if they were not to be eclipsed then the company had little option but to respond. It had taken almost four years, but the net result was that the Harland & Wolff shipyard at Belfast had been massively upgraded with two new giant slipways, and the Belfast Harbour Commissioners had constructed a brand-new graving dock to accommodate the new generation of White Star ships.

The original strategy had been to construct two giant vessels: *Olympic* and *Titanic*. These two ships would not only offer the height of luxury for passengers on the North Atlantic, but would also provide a new standard of service for the hundreds of thousands of European emigrants on their way to America. Although by no means capable of matching the Cunard sisters in terms of speed – White Star had long since given up that expensive pursuit – with a service speed of 21 knots, the Olympic-class ships were still fast and would be more than capable of maintaining a very respectable, comfortable and, most important of all, economic service between Southampton and New York.

Ismay's cable home that day did little to conceal his delight with the company's new vessel, describing *Olympic* as '… a marvel, and has given unbounded satisfaction', but in spite of his elation Ismay also knew that, although the White Star Line was once again in the ascendant, there was little time for the company to rest on its laurels. Cunard had scarcely been idle while White Star had forged ahead with the construction of *Olympic* and *Titanic*, and clearly aware of the potential of a ship of this class, they too had begun to explore the possibilities of constructing their own version. Less than a week after the launch of *Titanic*, the first keel plates of Cunard's *Aquitania* had already been laid, and with Albert Ballin's Hamburg America Line also planning an even larger trio

Britannic compared with St Paul's Cathedral. This was not an uncommon style of advertising at the time, helping to emphasise the ship's huge scale. (Author)

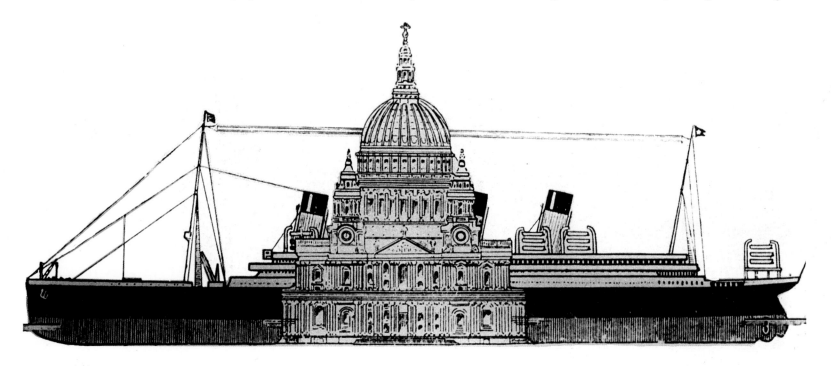

Due to the success of the first-class restaurant in *Olympic*, *Britannic*'s restaurant was expanded to run the entire width of the ship. (Author)

Britannic's first-class lounge would have been as sumptuous as those of her elder sisters. (Author)

of ships, the competition was already hot on the heels of the White Star Line.

Up to this point, a third Olympic-class vessel had simply not been an option for the White Star Line, but in the three years since *Olympic* and *Titanic* had been ordered the commercial realities had changed dramatically, and with the public response to the *Olympic* being so positive, the need to build a third ship of the class in order to comfortably maintain a weekly service between Southampton and New York became greater than ever.

It is against this background that *Britannic* was conceived. The contract for the ship's construction would not be finalised until 23 October 1911, but with both of the large slipways at Belfast already occupied, there was little need to rush. In the meantime, Harland & Wolff could begin to stockpile the materials and allocate the necessary resources, but on 28 June 1911, exactly one week after *Olympic* had arrived at New York, the official order to proceed was given.

At this stage Harland & Wolff probably envisaged building a third ship of the class which would in all probability have been a near-identical sister to *Olympic*, but even before the ship had returned to Southampton, Ismay was considering a number of improvements to be incorporated into *Titanic*. The most noticeable modifications would be a larger number of cabins along

Britannic's Turkish bath was a variation on a successful theme in *Olympic*. (Author)

the B deck promenade, which Ismay had noticed was under-utilised on *Olympic*'s maiden voyage. Other modifications would include a larger first-class restaurant, a veranda café and an enclosed forward A deck promenade, seemingly to take into account the sea spray in this area during more difficult crossings. Yet, in the main Ismay's modifications were based on any commercial and revenue-generating factors that his experienced eye could detect.

However, engineering factors beyond Ismay's area of expertise would oblige Harland & Wolff to consider further modifications to *Britannic*, which only closer study of the earlier vessels of the class could highlight. Throughout the summer of 1911 those lessons would be incorporated into *Titanic* while still fitting out at Belfast, but it would not be until the launch of the Royal Mail steamer *Arlanza* on 23 November 1911 that the necessary space needed for the construction of a third

Olympic-class liner was available; one week later, on 30 November, the keel of yard number 433, *Britannic*, was finally laid on slip no. 2 at Belfast.

Even at this early stage rumours of a fabulous new White Star vessel building at Belfast were beginning to circulate. On 25 November 1911, the *New York Times* had picked up on a story in the British press, speculating that the new ship – to be called *Gigantic* – would be 1,000ft long and 112ft wide. Intriguingly, the on-board facilities would include a cricket field, a tennis court, golf links and even a ballroom.

In actual fact, references to a White Star liner named *Gigantic* in the popular press were not new, and can even be traced as far back as the last decade of the nineteenth century, when another *Gigantic* was confidently predicted in the press. Ultimately that ship would indeed come to pass, although the *Gigantic* myth turned out to be just that when the 17,272grt *Oceanic* entered service.

The plunge baths in *Olympic* and *Titanic* were very utilitarian, but in *Britannic* the design was far more glamorous. (Author)

The origins of this *Gigantic* advertisement are obscure, but it has helped to maintain one of the great *Britannic* legends over the years. (Titanic Historical Society)

GIGANTIC, 1,000-FOOT LINER

To Have Golf Links, Cricket Field, Tennis Court, and Ballroom.

By Marconi Transatlantic Wireless Telegraph to The New York Times.

LONDON, Nov. 24, (by telegraph to Clifden, Ireland; thence by wireless.)— Remarkable details are now known of the thousand-foot liner, the Gigantic, which the White Star Line has commissioned Harland & Wolff to build at Belfast.

The beam will measure between 111 and 112 feet; the displacement will be 70,000 tons, and the gross tonnage over 50,000. The levels will be a dozen or thirteen, with the highest over seventy-five feet above the water line. The passenger accommodation will be increased in the first class from 800 to 1,000 or more, and the total passengers that can be carried will number over 4,000.

The Gigantic will not be an ocean greyhound, but a seven-day boat. She will have both reciprocating and turbine engines. The cost is to be close on to £2,000,000, or $10,000,000. She will have a cricket field, a tennis court, golf links, and reception and ball rooms, and restaurant and veranda cafés, which will be placed forward instead of aft. There will also be a plunge and all kinds of baths, and a gymnasium.

There will be a most elaborate scheme of decoration.

An early example of the *Gigantic* legend, in this particular case from the *New York Times*. (Bruce Beveridge)

Yard no. 433 would be no different in that respect, and nor for that matter did Harland & Wolff ever build another ship named *Gigantic* for any other client, but for reasons entirely beyond the control of the White Star publicity department, in more recent times there has been an attempt to re-write the already sensational history of *Titanic* by claiming that *Britannic*'s name was discreetly changed after the tragedy because the original choice was both pretentious and, in the unfortunate circumstances, also extremely embarrassing.

Embarrassing it would certainly have been, but the existing documentation tells a very different story. The *Gigantic* legend is admittedly attractive, but the inescapable fact is that all of the available working records at Harland & Wolff clearly show that the facts do not support it. Within the battered covers of the engineering records, each volume lists numerous vessels, all of them in numerical sequence as per their official yard number, and it can quite clearly be seen that at no time after the ship had been ordered is there any reference to the name *Gigantic*. Name changing was by no means unusual; indeed several other vessels on the same page as *Britannic* are recorded as having had their names changed during construction, but *Britannic* was not one of them. Cross-referenced with other relevant pages in several record books, the inescapable conclusion is that the first documented reference to the name *Britannic* at the Queen's Island works is logged as early as 28 June 1911 – less than a month after *Titanic* had been launched.

To this day, some persist in the belief that the ship's name was clandestinely changed, but the documented evidence all but disproves the theory. It is also unlikely that Harland & Wolff would have been involved in or been able to sustain any such cover-up. Then again, the shipbuilder was more concerned with yard numbers than a vessel's nomenclature, which would always remain a matter for the owners, but if there was ever any internal reference to the name *Gigantic* in the White Star publicity department prior to yard no. 433 being ordered, there is no known official written record.

It was not uncommon for a ship's name to be altered during the construction phase, but this particular record from Harland & Wolff clearly shows that no such change was ever considered for *Britannic*. (Harland & Wolff/PRONI)

Another Harland & Wolff record book details the progress of *Britannic*'s construction. Again, there is no record of any change in nomenclature. (Harland & Wolff/PRONI)

General arrangement plans of RMS *Britannic*, as designed for service on the North Atlantic mail run. The ship incorporated the most successful elements in *Olympic* and *Titanic*, with the revised B deck layout being particularly noticeable. (*Engineering* magazine)

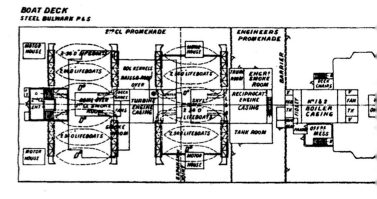

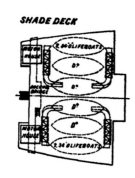

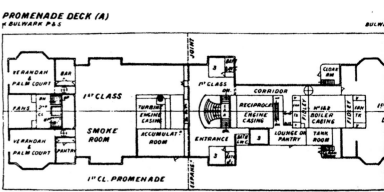

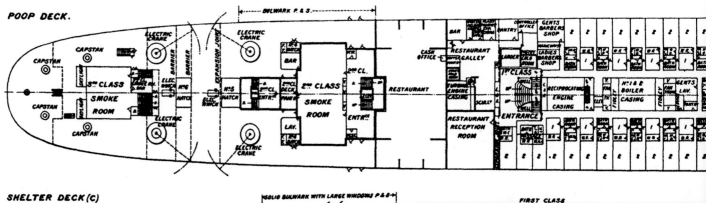

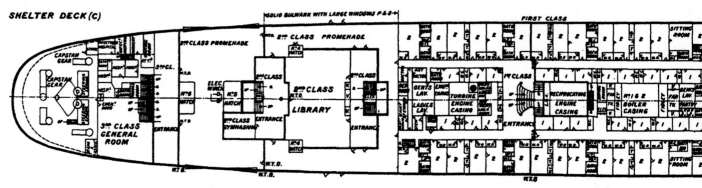

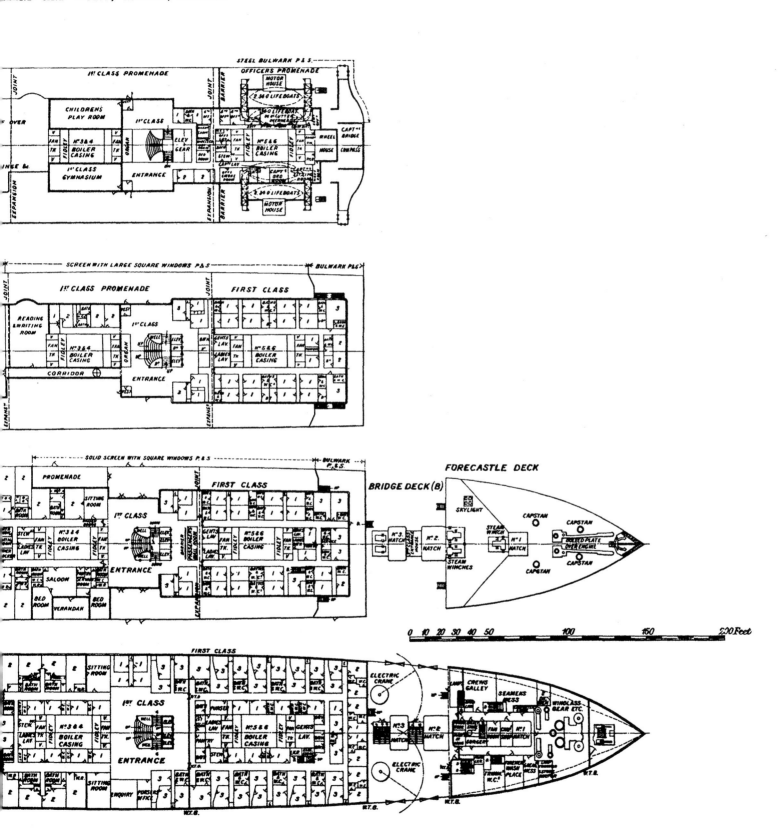

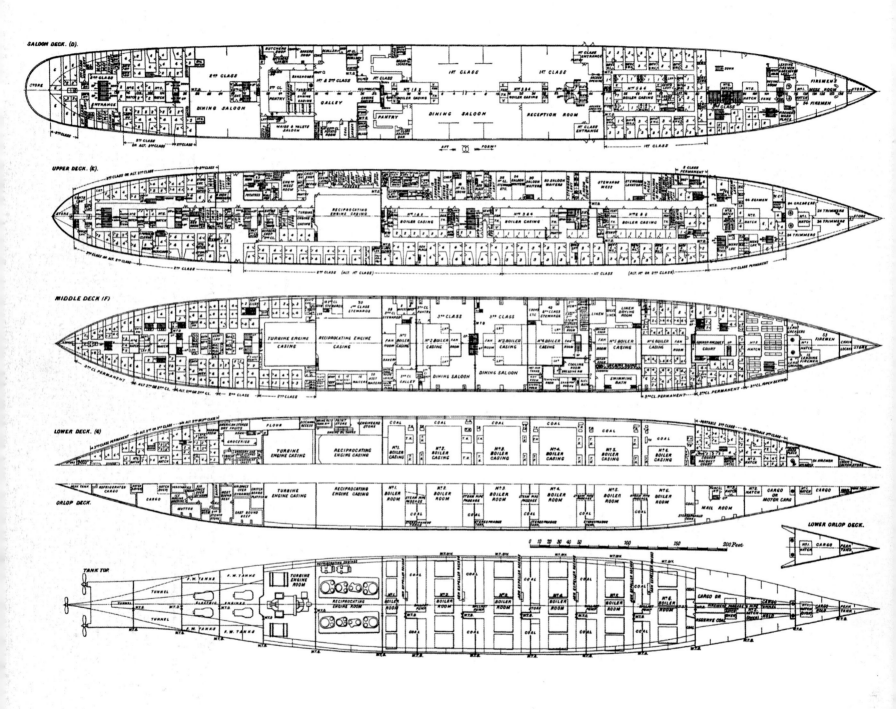

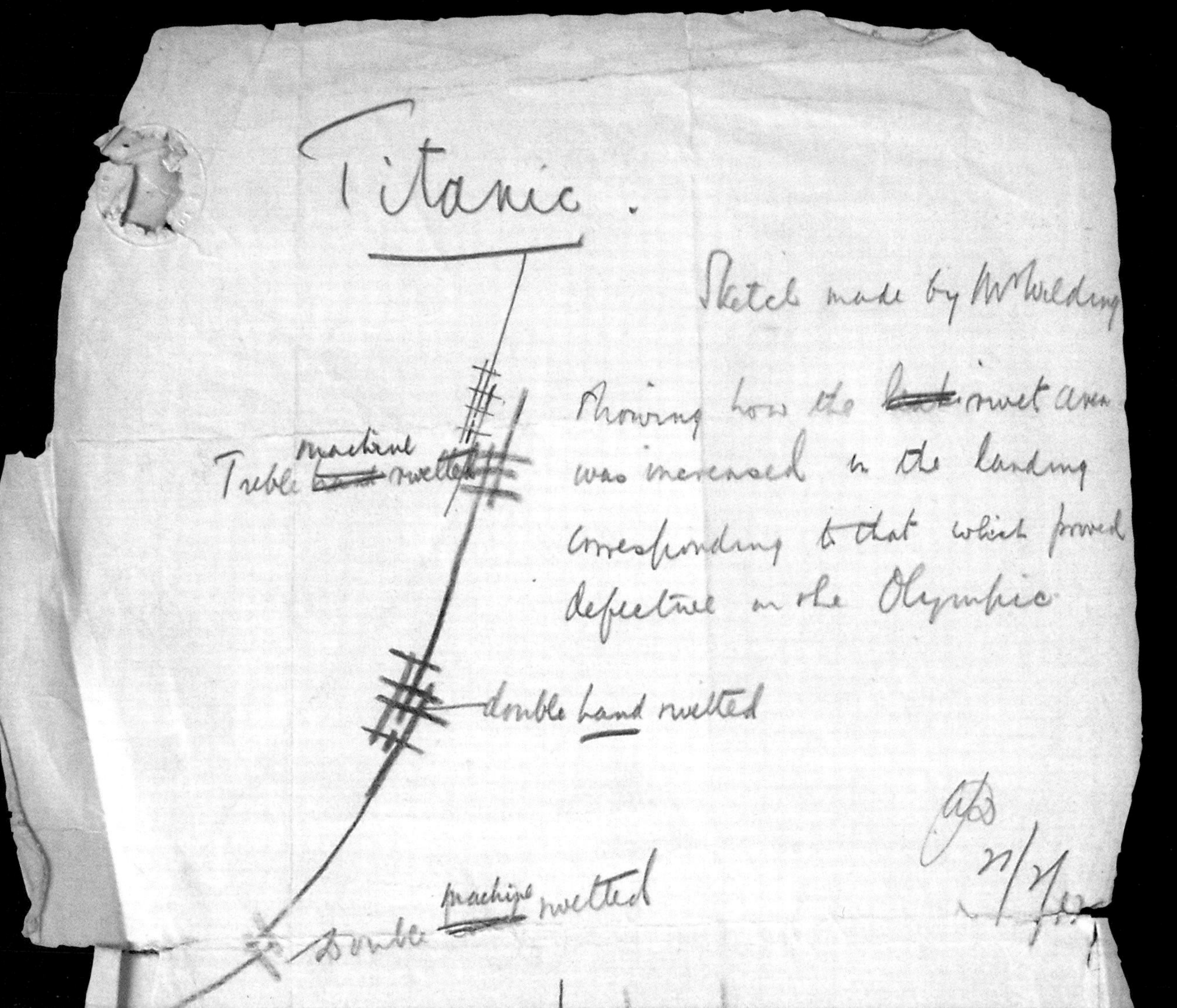

Titanic.

Sketch made by Mr Wilding

showing how the ~~rivet~~ rivet area was increased in the landing corresponding to that which proved defective in the *Olympic.*

Treble machine ~~rivetted~~ rivetted

double hand rivetted

double machine rivetted

A sketch from January 1912 made by Edward Wilding, emphasising a weakness in *Olympic*'s riveted seams. (National Archives)

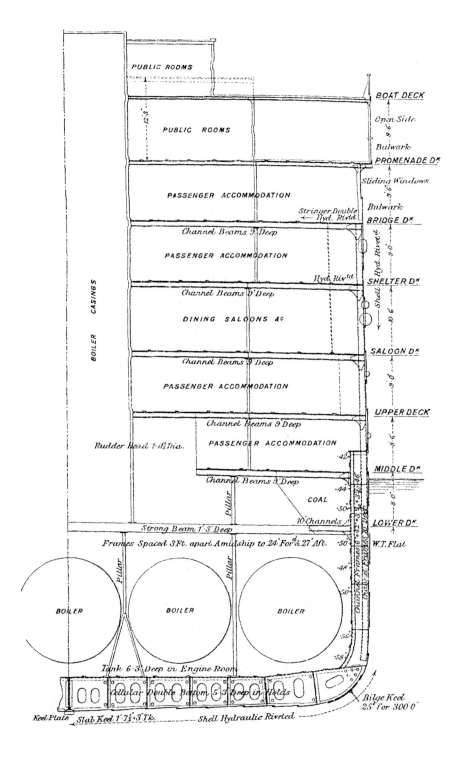

PUBLIC ROOMS

BOAT DECK

Open Side

PUBLIC ROOMS

12'3"

Bulwark

PROMENADE Dᵏ

Sliding Windows

PASSENGER ACCOMMODATION

Stringer Double Hyd. Rivtd

Bulwark

9'6"

BRIDGE Dᵏ

Channel Beams 9 Deep

Hyd. Rivtd

PASSENGER ACCOMMODATION

Shell Hyd. Rivtd

9'6"

SHELTER Dᵏ

BOILER CASINGS

Channel Beams 9 Deep

DINING SALOONS &ᶜ

9'6"

SALOON Dᵏ

Channel Beams 9 Deep

PASSENGER ACCOMMODATION

9'6"

UPPER DECK

Channel Beams 9 Deep

Rudder Head 1·1½ Dia.

PASSENGER ACCOMMODATION

9'6"

·42"

MIDDLE Dᵏ

Channel Beams 3 Deep

Pillar

COAL

·44"

·50"

10 Channels

8'0"

LOWER Dᵏ

Strong Beam 1'3 Deep

·50"

W.T. Flat

Frames Spaced 3 Ft. apart Amidship to 24 Forᵈ & 27 Aft.

·48"

Pillar

Pillar

Pillar

·50"

BOILER

BOILER

BOILER

·56"

·58"

Tank 6·3 Deep in Engine Room

Cellular Double Bottom 5·5 Deep in Holds

Bilge Keel 25" for 300'0"

Keel Plate

Slab Keel 1'7½·3 Tk.

Shell Hydraulic Riveted

Although at first sight *Britannic's* mid-ship profile looks almost identical to that of *Olympic* and *Titanic*, the invisible double skin running alongside the ship bears silent testimony to the disaster that had overwhelmed *Titanic*. (Author)

The initial pace of the work on *Britannic* was swift enough, with the hull being framed to the height of the double bottom by 12 March 1912, but already behind the scenes a number of issues were beginning to materialise. In January 1912, *Olympic* had experienced a particularly heavy Atlantic crossing which had highlighted serious issues in a number of the ship's riveted seams; when the vessel was dry-docked at the beginning of March 1912 in order to have a propeller blade replaced, the opportunity was therefore taken to replace and strengthen a number of riveted seams. The additional strengthening was also carried out to the riveting alongside the turbine engine room and Boiler Room 6 in *Titanic*. Furthermore, a number of small cracks were observed in the superstructure in the vicinity of some of the deck houses at the level of B deck, and also in the vicinity of the aft expansion joints. It was the first sign that perhaps all was not well with the design of the Olympic-class vessels, but although this was not necessarily to be unexpected in view of the huge technological leap that Harland & Wolff had taken, even at this early stage the learning curve in the operation of *Olympic* and the soon-to-be-completed *Titanic* would result in a number of significant redesigns in *Britannic*.

To an untrained eye, these modifications would not have been strikingly obvious. Nevertheless, even by January 1912 the evident movement and flexing in *Olympic's* hull, along with the evident fatigue being caused by the flexing in the top structure, was of enough concern for *Britannic's* engineering records to include an important modification, increasing the breadth of the vessel by 18in. At some later date, a further modification would also be made to *Britannic's* superstructure, which would incorporate three expansion joints instead of the two in *Olympic* and *Titanic* in order to help distribute the topside flexing over as large an area as possible.

But all of this was as nothing compared to what came next.

Less than two weeks after departing from Belfast, shortly before midnight on 14 April 1912, RMS *Titanic* struck an iceberg on her maiden voyage. Two hours and twenty minutes later the ship disappeared beneath the surface of an unusually tranquil Atlantic Ocean, taking with her 1,503 passengers and crew. As the 712 dazed

Slip no. 2 in April 1913, by which time *Britannic* was fully framed. (Harland & Wolff)

By October 1913 *Britannic*'s
hull was fully framed and work
could begin on the hull plating.
(Harland & Wolff)

survivors were landed at New York the world was already hungry for answers and the Americans would waste no time, with Joseph Bruce Ismay being called before the Senate Committee Inquiry being chaired by William Alden Smith, the Republican senator for Michigan. Smith acted quickly and his report was completed less than six weeks after the disaster, with Lord Mersey's British report following two months later. Each report was strikingly different in many ways, but the overall conclusions in both were undeniable: Smith and Mersey agreed on the crucial steps that needed to be taken in order to ensure greater safety at sea, with both recommending increased watertight subdivision and, more importantly, sufficient lifeboat capacity for everyone on board.

Lord Mersey's report would not be published until 30 July 1912, but long before either document was in the public domain both the White Star Line and Harland & Wolff would be crunching numbers of their own in order to restore their battered reputations. It didn't need any public investigation to highlight the lack of lifeboat capacity and, for the time being, White Star could take steps to ensure that adequate temporary lifeboat capacity could be installed in *Olympic*, although that was of little benefit in the short term as the stokehold crew, uncertain of the safety of the additional collapsible lifeboats, mutinied on 24 April and declined to sail on the ship's next scheduled crossing from Southampton to New York. Unable to reach a compromise, two days later the voyage

Britannic's cellular double skin, designed to ensure that if damaged then the water would be kept confined to a smaller area of the ship's side. (Harland & Wolff)

In the six boiler rooms, arranged as in *Olympic* and *Titanic*, there were twenty-four double-ended and five single-ended boilers, with a total of 159 furnaces. In *Britannic* the double-ended boilers were 1ft longer, giving them a slightly larger heating surface of 5,702sq. ft. The combined 159 furnaces accounted for a total grate area of 3,461sq. ft and 150,958sq. ft of heating surface – a ratio of 1:43.6. (Author)

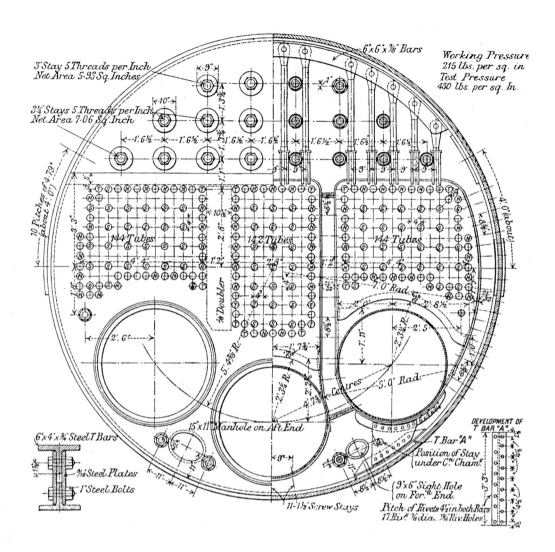

A starboard profile of *Britannic*, emphasising the higher and more numerous bulkheads and the double skin along the engine and boiler room spaces. (Author)

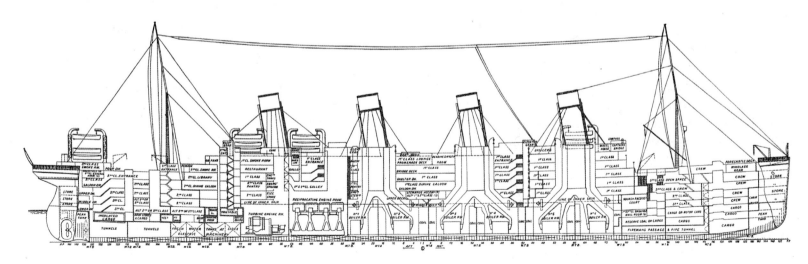

was cancelled altogether and *Olympic* remained at Southampton until her next scheduled crossing on 15 May.

As far as *Britannic* was concerned, the uncertainty was even greater, with rumours circulating that White Star would cancel the project altogether. However, the commercial realities rendered such an option unlikely. No matter how great the disaster, there was no way that White Star could maintain a balanced express service between Southampton and New York with the *Oceanic* and the ageing *Majestic* running in tandem with *Olympic*. On the other hand, it was also clear that wholesale alterations in certain aspects of the ship's design would need to be reconsidered.

Work on yard no. 433 was subsequently slowed, but a closer look at the modified building schedule shows that the delay was not especially severe. *Britannic* would be fully framed by 27 February 1913, approximately fifty weeks after completing the framing to the double bottom; however, considering that it had taken forty-six weeks between completing the framing in *Titanic*'s double bottom to the completion of the hull framing, in reality we are only talking of a difference of about four weeks.

Behind the scenes, however, the Harland & Wolff drawing offices were working overtime. Externally it would take a trained eye to spot the subtle structural differences of the third and, as it would turn out, final Olympic-class liner, but internally *Britannic* would be a very different ship. An extra bulkhead was added in the electric engine room, dividing the ship into seventeen compartments, as opposed to the sixteen in *Olympic* and *Titanic*, but more importantly five of these bulkheads now extended as far up as the bridge deck. To further add to *Britannic*'s unsinkability credentials, a double skin would run alongside all six of the ship's boiler rooms, as well as the reciprocating and turbine engine rooms, for a total length of 447ft. This alone amounted to over half the length of the ship (between perpendiculars), although if including the freshwater tanks aft of the turbine engine space, then the length of the double skin amounted to over 60 per cent of the ship's length. All of these factors combined would also add significantly to the stiffness and strength of the ship's hull.

As 1912 drifted into 1913, *Britannic* steadily grew on the stocks. By 20 September 1913 the hull was fully plated,

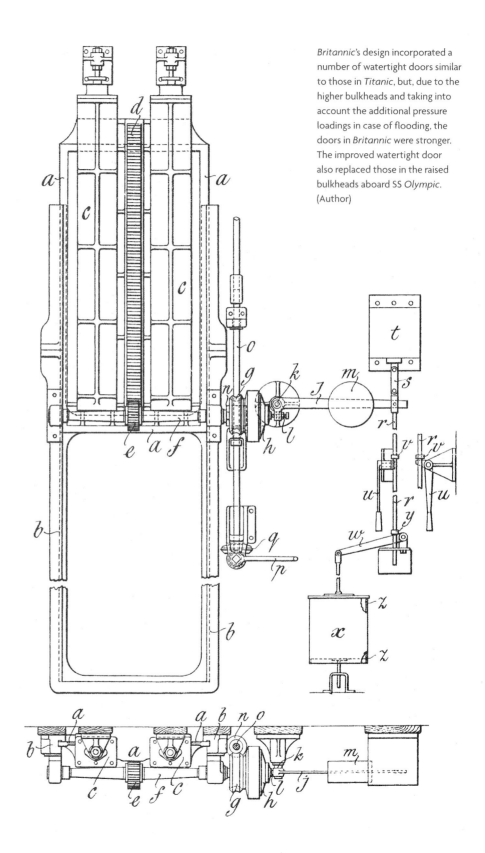

Britannic's design incorporated a number of watertight doors similar to those in *Titanic*, but, due to the higher bulkheads and taking into account the additional pressure loadings in case of flooding, the doors in *Britannic* were stronger. The improved watertight door also replaced those in the raised bulkheads aboard SS *Olympic*. (Author)

but, while structurally the ship was significantly different to the original design, at the same time much of the internal working layout of the ship would be identical to that in *Olympic* and *Titanic*. The six boiler rooms still contained twenty-four double-ended and five single-ended boilers, with a total of 159 furnaces; the only real difference was that in *Britannic* the double-ended boilers were 1ft longer. The engine room arrangements were also practically identical, with two four-cylinder inverted triple-expansion reciprocating engines exhausting into a low-pressure turbine. The original Olympic-class design had called for the turbine to be used only once the ship was in open water, but subsequent experience in *Olympic* had shown that the vessel's steering qualities were considerably improved when using the central propeller

to manoeuvre in enclosed waters, and this practice had quickly become the norm.

The design of *Britannic*'s turbine engine, however, was considerably different. The turbine in *Britannic* had been designed and constructed by Harland & Wolff, whereas those in *Olympic* and *Titanic* had been built by John Brown & Co. Essentially they were the same in that they could only operate when the ship was steaming ahead, but the real difference was in their size and power; the turbine in *Olympic* weighed 420 tons and could develop 16,000hp, whereas the 490-ton turbine in *Britannic* was capable of developing 18,000hp. All of this machinery combined meant that, with a total of 50,000hp, *Britannic* was more than capable of maintaining her designed service speed of 21 knots.

The Olympic-class reciprocating engines were of the four-cylinder triple-expansion type, balanced on the Yarrow-Schlick-Tweedy system, with the low-pressure cylinders placed at both ends of the engine for the purpose of balancing. The diameters of the cylinders were 54in, 84in and two at 97in; the length of stroke was 75in. (Author)

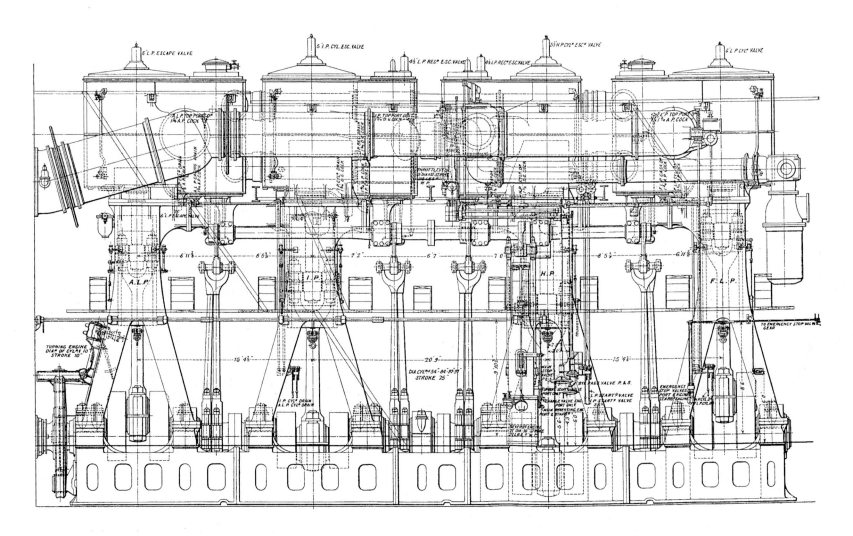

To the travelling public, *Britannic* would also incorporate the best features in *Olympic* and *Titanic*. Although near-identical sister ships in many ways, there were still subtle differences in each vessel to tell them apart. Already mentioned was the open promenade on B deck in *Olympic*, which Bruce Ismay had opted to fill with additional cabins in *Titanic*, but *Britannic*'s internal arrangements would essentially be a hybrid version of the two earlier ships, with the open B deck promenade remaining in situ as far back as the forward first-class entrance. Aft of this point the open promenade would be filled by additional cabin space, including the two millionaires' suites, each with their own private promenade, which had subsequently been incorporated into *Titanic*. However, one of the key differences further aft was the

first-class restaurant, which had proved so popular in *Olympic*; *Britannic*'s restaurant would stretch from port to starboard, whereas in *Titanic*, and subsequently in the modified *Olympic*, a Café Parisien had been installed on the starboard side of B deck. In *Britannic* there would be no such café, with the builders instead opting for the two existing veranda cafés on the aft boat deck. As in *Titanic*, *Britannic*'s forward promenade on A deck would also be enclosed with sliding windows, whereas in *Olympic* this modification would never be installed – in all likelihood because *Olympic*'s post-*Titanic* boat deck did not enjoy the same unobstructed views as that of *Britannic*.

Other alterations to the internal arrangements included the addition of a children's playroom on the port boat deck, a hairdressing salon for the ladies next to the

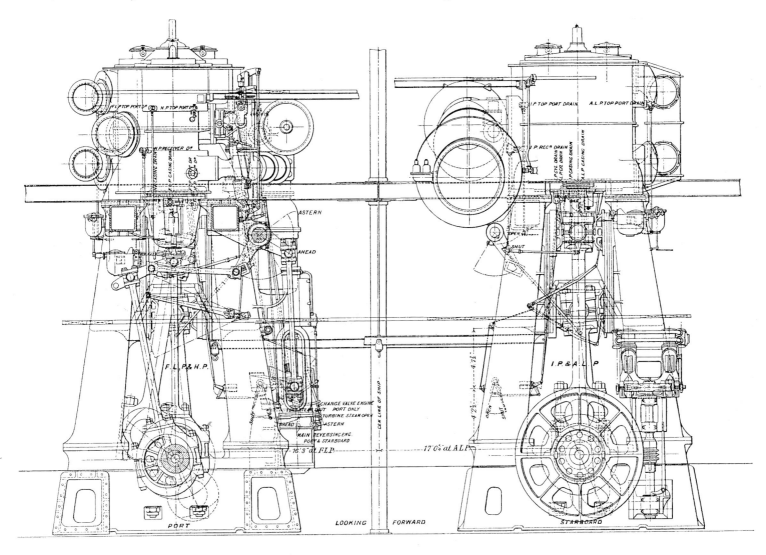

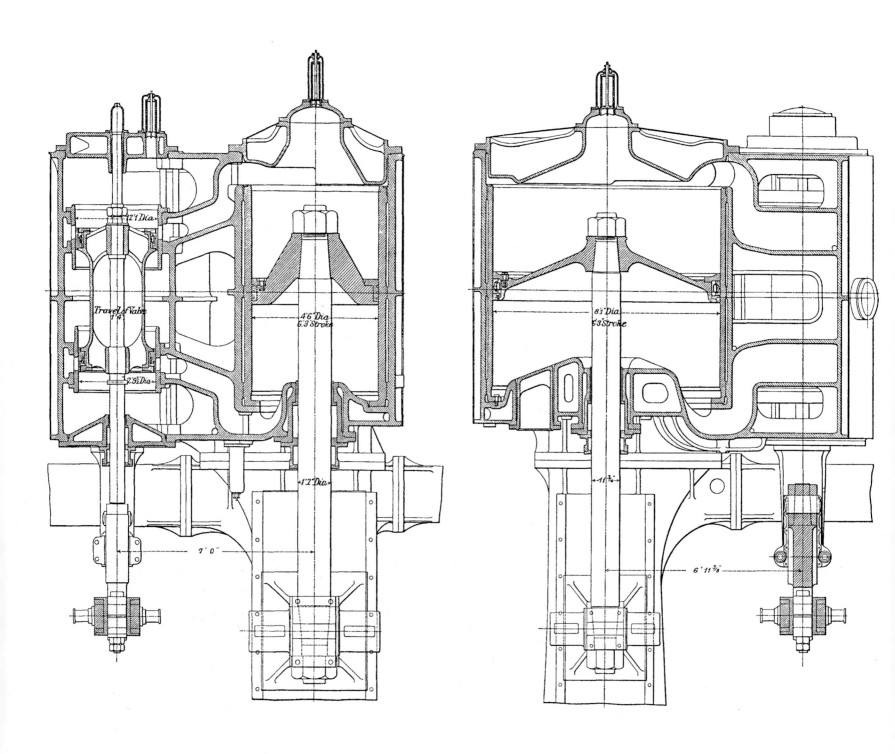

gentlemen's barber on B deck, an additional first-class elevator amidships and even an organ in the main first-class entrance. But perhaps the most attractive option for the travelling public was the fact that *Britannic* would also have a larger proportion of cabins with private bathrooms, each with improved internal plumbing so that hot water could be pumped through almost as soon as the tap was turned on.

There was, however, one undeniable difference in the design of the three ships. *Olympic* and *Titanic* had originally been fitted with a single line of lifeboats along the forward and aft ends of their port and starboard boat decks. The loss of *Titanic* had highlighted the lack of lifeboat capacity, but while White Star had corrected this deficiency in *Olympic* by virtually enclosing the boat deck with a line of Welin double-acting lifeboat davits – fourteen sets on each side of the ship and each capable of handling one rigid and one collapsible lifeboat – in *Britannic* the builders had opted for an altogether different approach.

There could be no doubt that safety had been made an absolute priority in *Britannic* and any passenger staring at the planned eight sets of huge lattice-girder davits would have little reason to doubt it. The February 1914 edition of *Engineering* magazine wrote that the davits could accommodate forty-eight lifeboats – although subsequent designs would indicate that the number had been reduced to forty-four – pointing out that the huge size of the davits would enable them to lower the 34ft lifeboats close to or, if necessary due to any list, at a greater distance from the side of ship. The stacked lifeboat arrangements on tiers at strategic areas of the boat deck also meant that the passengers could take their place in the lifeboats on the relative safety of the deck before the davits could lift the fully loaded lifeboats over the side. Two of the boats would also be equipped with their own engines and wireless.

The day inevitably came when Harland & Wolff could do no more on the shore. After twenty-seven months

The turbine driving the centre shaft was of the Parsons exhaust type, designed to take steam from the two reciprocating engines at a pressure of about 10lb absolute, exhausting into two condensers. The overall length of the turbine was about 50ft; the rotor blade weighed 150 tons, while the total weight of the turbine complete was 490 tons. (Diagrams opposite: Author; below: Harland & Wolff)

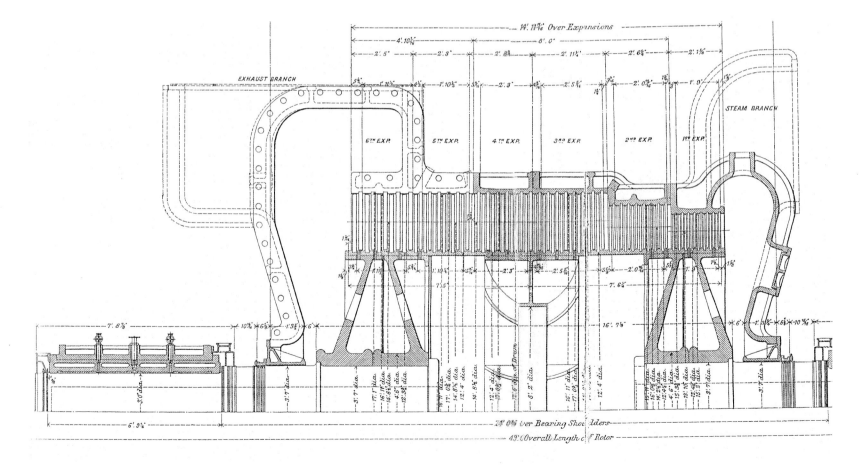

PLAN OF ROTOR SHEWING LEFT HAND BLADING.

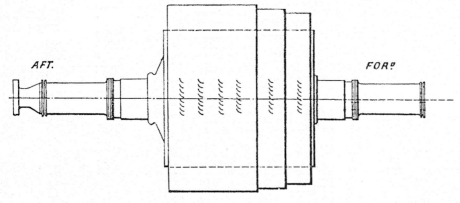

AFT.   FOR?

PLAN OF BOTTOM OF CYLINDER SHEWING
LEFT HAND BLADING.

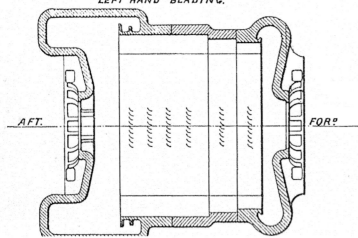

AFT.   FOR?

ship's bow as she slid down the ways; there was simply the White Star company flag flying above the gantry with signal flags beneath spelling out the word 'Success'.

The river Lagan beside slip no. 2 was deep enough to allow *Britannic* a launch run of anything up to 2,350ft, but it was unlikely that she would need all of this. Instead of being placed on each side of the berth, the drags, consisting of three anchors and masses of chain on each side of the ship, were laid in the water. Each was strategically placed so that the checks of the wire ropes secured to the shell of the ship came into play after the bow of the vessel had travelled a short distance from the end of the standing ways. In spite of the extensive technical preparations, the yard foremen were still obliged to closely watch the river to ensure the highest possible tide before the first rocket was fired at 11.10 a.m. to signal the workmen to knock away the few remaining blocks supporting the keel; the rocket also warned any vessels on the river to stand clear, as by that time only the steel hydraulic launching triggers were holding the ship on the slipway. As a second rocket was fired at 11.15 a.m. the triggers were released and, needing no assistance from the hydraulic rams, *Britannic*'s grey-painted hull moved down the slipway, the passage made easier by over 20 tons of tallow, train oil and soft soap. Eighty-one seconds later, having reached a speed of 9.5 knots, *Britannic* was afloat, the drags having brought the hull safely to a halt before it had travelled its entire length in the water.

The reporter from *Engineering* magazine described the event in more detail:

on the slipway, *Britannic* was finally ready for launching on 26 February 1914. Considering the traumas of the hull's development, it is scarcely believable that this was only one month longer than it had taken *Titanic* to reach the launching stage, although comparisons with *Olympic*'s twenty-two months from keel laying to launch are probably unfair considering that both the White Star Line and Harland & Wolff had given the earlier vessel total priority.

Continuing a longstanding White Star tradition, the occasion demanded a glittering guest list, including the company bigwigs, Admiralty officials and local Belfast dignitaries, but for all that there was no real launching ceremony as such. Even though the customary Belfast weather added little to the occasion, there was no White Star tradition of breaking a bottle of champagne on the

The launch was carried out in calm but wet weather, and was in every way successful. The pressure on the hydraulic ram of the trigger arrangement attained a maximum of 560 tons, and on this being released the ship moved at once; the hydraulic starting-jacks were not required. The time which expired from the beginning of movement until the vessel was afloat was 81 seconds, the maximum speed attained being 9½ knots. The stern dip was 31 ft., and the stem dip 17 ft. The draught of the vessel when afloat was 15 ft. 4½ in. forward and 25 ft. 7 in. aft, which corresponds to a displacement weight of 24,800 tons. The vessel was afterwards berthed for

Right and far right (top): *Britannic*'s philharmonic organ would have dominated the forward first-class main entrance. The philharmonic was actually developed through 'crossing' orchestrions with console-played organs, and were thus playable either by an organist or through a built-in roll playing apparatus, similar to a player-piano. (right: Author; far right (top): Harland & Wolff)

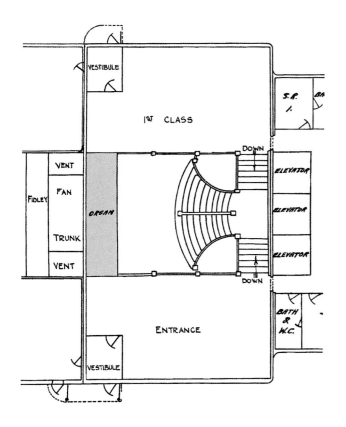

completion at a deep-water wharf belonging to the harbour authorities, and there the 200-ton floating crane belonging to Messrs. Harland and Wolff will be placed between the ship and the wharf when required for shipping the machinery, rafts being constructed to keep the ship the required distance from the wharf at the forward and after ends.

One of the yard workers, however, was less impressed by the technical detail, preferring to comment rather more succinctly: 'They just builds 'er and shoves 'er in.'

Following the launch, the dignitaries retired to Belfast's Grand Central Hotel for the customary speeches and lunch, but for the shipyard workers there was no time for any such diversions. Like any other Thursday, they had a great deal of work to get done before they would be allowed home, not least the prospect of clearing the now empty slip no. 2 in preparation for Harland & Wolff's next contract, the Red Star liner *Nederland*, better known in the shipyard as yard no. 469.

For *Britannic*, the immediate future involved another six months alongside the deep-water fitting-out wharf, but if everything went according to plan then with luck she could still be in service by the late autumn.

Below: The final 1914 rigging plan for *Britannic*'s commercial design indicates the reduced number of lifeboats placed beneath the forward sets of davits. The outboard cutters would also be removed from the eventual boat complement. (Harland & Wolff)

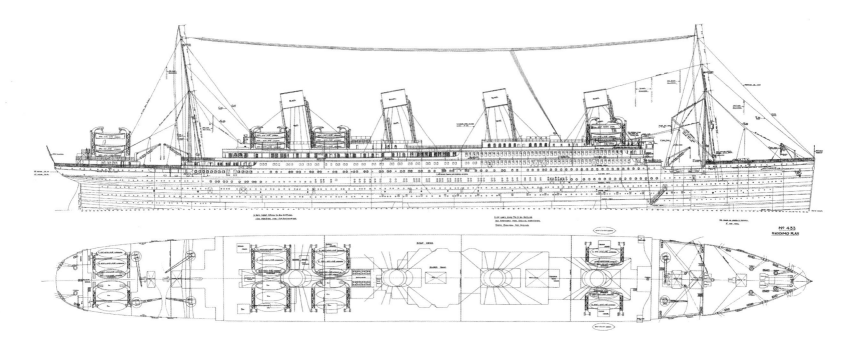

Top & middle: Due to the stiffness of the superstructure in *Olympic*, the flexing tended to concentrate in the area of the strength deck below at the position of the expansion joints. An additional expansion joint incorporated into *Britannic*'s superstructure would allow this flexing to be distributed over a larger area. (Harland & Wolff)

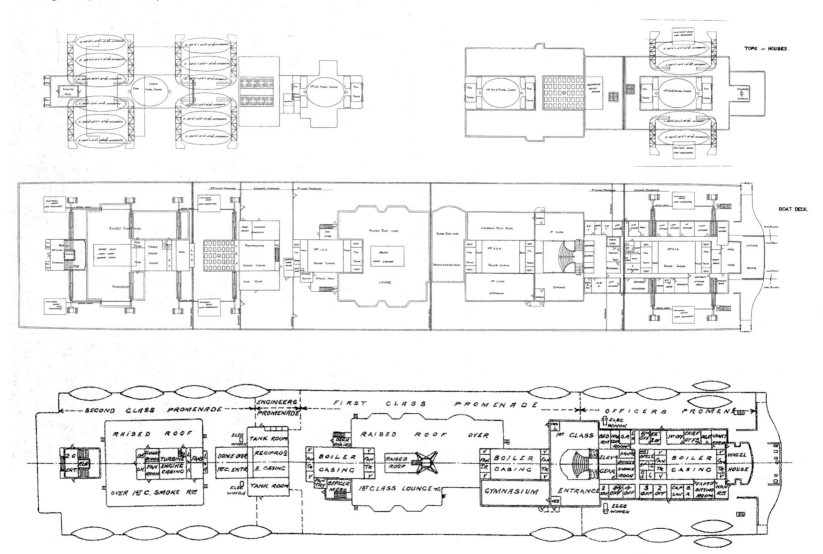

Bottom: The boat deck arrangements in *Olympic* and *Titanic*. (Author)

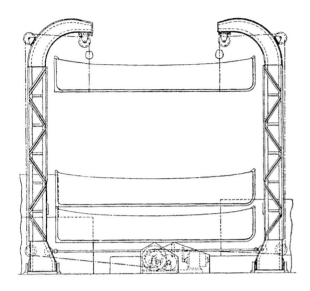

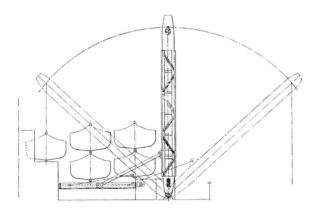

Designed by William Edward Armstrong, *Britannic*'s lifeboat davits were of a lattice-girder construction and of much greater height than those generally used even in the larger ships of the day. The davits were mounted like shear-legs on horizontal pivots sufficiently far apart to let the 34ft lifeboats pass between them, making it possible to lower the boats at a greater distance from the ship in the event of a list. The lifeboats were arranged in several tiers across the deck and if necessary could be traversed across the deck and operated by the davits on the opposite side of the ship. (Diagrams above: Author; right: Bruce Beveridge Collection)

RMS *Britannic* after launching on 26 February 1914. (Harland & Wolff)

3

WAR

Less than a month after the launch *Britannic*'s boilers were already being hoisted aboard. (Harland & Wolff)

When *Britannic* had been launched it was anticipated that she would enter service in September 1914, but due to a combination of supply, financial and workforce issues at Belfast the schedule began to slip. In July 1914 it was announced that *Britannic* would not be ready for her maiden voyage until the spring of 1915, which although disappointing for the White Star Line, would almost certainly have come as a welcome relief for Harland & Wolff, which at this time was already stretched to full capacity.

History, however, had other plans, and during the summer of 1914 the pillars that had kept the peace in Europe for almost a hundred years began to fall. On 28 June 1914, the Austrian archduke Franz Ferdinand was assassinated in Sarajevo in Serbia, but hostilities did not really begin until one month later, when Austria Hungary invaded Serbia on 28 July. Great Britain had initially hoped to remain on the sidelines, but when Russia sided with Serbia and Germany declared its support for Austria, the die was cast. France declared its support for Russia and,

when Germany marched into neutral Belgium on 4 August in violation of the Treaty of London, Britain's guarantee of Belgian neutrality left the British Government with no alternative but to declare war on Germany. By 3 November 1914, Great Britain and France were also at war with Germany's ally Turkey, and by the end of 1914 the hostilities looked likely to continue for the foreseeable future. In spite of the initial high hopes, there was no longer any chance of the fighting being over by Christmas.

The impact of the hostilities was no less apparent at Belfast. Harland & Wolff was not in the business of building warships, and with the majority of raw materials suddenly diverted to shipyards with Admiralty contracts, there was little option but to slow the work on the many civil contracts until the immediate supply problems had stabilised. The fact that many trained shipyard workers had also rushed to enlist was also creating numerous manpower problems, so the likelihood of *Britannic* being completed in the short term was unlikely. In spite of the logistical headaches, however, work was still far enough advanced by September 1914 for the ship to be

Britannic laid up incomplete at Belfast following the outbreak of war. Beside her lie two smaller merchant vessels being converted into dummy battleships. (Bruce Beveridge)

By April 1914 the bed plates for the reciprocating engines were ready for the engine cylinders. (Harland & Wolff)

placed in the Thompson graving dock in order to have her propellers fitted. Nevertheless, even this was just a short respite, as the first Admiralty orders finally began to arrive at Belfast that October for the conversion of a number of merchant vessels into dummy battleships.

Whether the White Star Line liked it or not, *Britannic* was simply not seen as a priority, although as passenger traffic between Europe and America had already been dramatically reduced, there was little call for a ship of her size anyway. With Southampton commandeered for military use, an improvised IMM service was still maintained between Liverpool and New York, while *Olympic* continued to operate from the relative safety of Greenock, on the Clyde. But even this would prove a temporary arrangement, and until the passenger numbers were considered high enough to justify the use of such large vessels, it was inevitable that the decision would be taken to withdraw *Olympic* from service. Her last eastbound crossing commenced on 21 October 1914, but the voyage was interrupted on the morning of Tuesday the 27th when the vessel ran into the 2nd Battle Squadron off the north coast of Ireland, where the British battleship HMS *Audacious* had been seriously damaged by a German mine. Answering the calls for assistance, *Olympic* succeeded in evacuating *Audacious*' crew, and at one time even took the damaged battleship in tow, but the elements combined to thwart the attempts to save the stricken vessel when, shortly before 9 p.m. that night, *Audacious*' forward magazine exploded. Rather than complete her voyage to the Clyde, for security reasons *Olympic* was ordered into the British naval base at Lough Swilly before returning directly to Belfast on 3 November.

The completed 1915 rigging plan of *Britannic* in the clearly identifiable colours of a hospital ship. (Harland & Wolff)

For the next ten months *Olympic* and *Britannic* would remain secured at Belfast, seemingly forgotten though never totally out of mind. The simple fact, however, was that the Admiralty had no great desire to utilise the larger liners as their deep draughts, ability to burn huge amounts of coal and the need for such large crews to service them made them totally unsuitable – not to mention hopelessly uneconomic – for patrol duties in coastal waters. As armed merchant cruisers the larger passenger vessels had been shown to be an undoubted failure, and the Director of Transports at the War Office made clear in no uncertain terms exactly why they were of no practical use, writing:

These ships will accommodate large numbers – between 5,000 and 6,000 men each – but the risk of loss from submarine attack, owing to their great size and impossibility of taking them into closed harbours, is only justifiable if the emergency warrants it being taken.

The Allied invasion of Gallipoli in April 1915 would change everything, and the sudden need for large numbers of troops to be transported to the Mediterranean meant that the larger vessels could no longer be overlooked. Of equal importance to the War Office, the benefits of converting one large ship as opposed to four or five smaller ones, which were needed elsewhere anyway, could not be denied. The big ships were ideally suited for the task of transporting large numbers of troops and, by June 1915, *Mauretania* and *Aquitania* had both been requisitioned for trooping duties to the Dardanelles. The large volumes

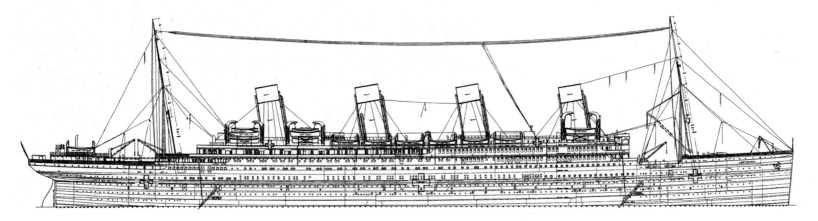

of casualties also meant that within three months both of these vessels had been converted to hospital ships, with the result that *Olympic* was also requisitioned as a troopship on 1 September. With the unrelenting pressure in the Mediterranean, on 13 November 1915 the War Office finally accepted the inevitable and official word was received at Belfast that *Britannic* was urgently required for service as a hospital ship.

As it happened, work on *Britannic* was already quite far advanced. Although by no means complete, work on the ship's wooden panelling and fittings was well under way, even if none of the luxury furnishings had been installed. But more importantly, the mooring trials of the engines had already been completed six months earlier, and Harland & Wolff were confident that the ship could be made ready within four weeks.

Even so, the pace was still frantic as the fitters worked to complete the ship's plumbing, electrics and galleys, while at the same time carpenters completely reworked the interior of the ship by installing 3,309 bunks, mostly of the two-tier type, for the invalids. Externally the ship also underwent a complete facelift, with six sets of Welin davits being fitted along both sides of the boat deck in place of three of the larger sets of girder davits that had yet to be installed. To complete the effect, the paint crews had also completely transformed the exterior, with the hull painted in the internationally recognised colours of a hospital ship: white with a green band along the hull, broken by three red crosses. Also, to ensure the ship's safety at night, a line of green lights ran beneath the promenade deck, while two electric red crosses were fitted on either side of the boat deck, each lit by 125 electric light bulbs.

By 6 December 1915, work was far enough advanced for the Admiralty to officially inform the German authorities via neutral channels in Holland of *Britannic*'s status as a military hospital ship, and on the 8th *Britannic* finally proceeded into Belfast Lough and the Irish Sea to complete her sea trials. As with *Titanic*, *Britannic*'s trials lasted a single day, although the vessel's return later that evening into the foggy confines of Belfast Lough created huge anxiety for the tugs waiting to assist her back into port. No official data surrounding *Britannic*'s trials was ever released, but they must have been successful as the

At the age of 43, Captain Charles Alfred Bartlett was one of the White Star Line's most experienced skippers. His last command for the company had been RMS *Cedric*, before coming ashore in January 1912 to assume the post of White Star Line Marine Superintendent at Liverpool. His shore-based duties would also have involved him overseeing *Titanic*'s fitting out. (Alasdair Fairbairn Collection)

Lieutenant Colonel Henry Stewart Anderson was appointed as *Britannic*'s senior medical officer on 21 December 1915, barely a day before the ship departed from Liverpool on her maiden voyage. His sixteen years in the corps had seen service in South Africa, India and Egypt. Anderson went to France as early as 18 August 1914, attached to the 1st Battalion North Staffordshire Regiment before being invalided home in January 1915. (Author)

Harland & Wolff engineering records confirm that the ship was duly handed over that same day. On the evening of 11 December 1915, a little over four years after her keel had been laid, *Britannic* finally departed from Belfast under the command of Captain Joseph Ranson, arriving at Liverpool's Gladstone Dock the following morning, where she was immediately commissioned as a military hospital ship.

The White Star Line's original choice of commander for *Britannic* had been Captain Herbert James Haddock, who had commanded *Olympic* before the war and had distinguished himself in the attempted rescue of HMS *Audacious*. The Admiralty, believing that Haddock was of more value in his post at Belfast co-ordinating the conversion of merchant vessels into dummy battleships, were reluctant to release him from his duties and, on 14 December, Captain Charles Alfred Bartlett, late commander of the Admiralty yacht *Verona* and, prior to the war, White Star Marine Superintendent at Liverpool since 1912, officially relieved Ranson as *Britannic*'s captain.

Aboard the 437-ton *Verona*, Bartlett's responsibilities had extended to co-ordinating the patrolling and minesweeping activities in the North Sea off Aberdeen, but *Britannic* would be a very different matter. Fortunately he was no stranger to big ships, having commanded White Star's 21,035grt *Cedric* for five years before assuming his shore-based position at Liverpool.

Captain Bartlett's previous command had been the 437-ton HMY *Verona*. From this yacht he would co-ordinate a fleet of trawlers which, disguised as fishing boats, would regularly sweep the approaches to the British naval base at Scapa Flow for mines. On 5 June 1915 the flotilla even succeeded in snagging the German submarine *U14* in their nets, forcing the U-boat to the surface before sinking it. (Alasdair Fairbairn Collection)

Britannic at Mudros. (TBF)

The clientele would be somewhat different to those that he had conveyed in the past, but for the next nine days Bartlett set about overseeing the final preparations as the last of the medical supplies and surgical equipment were placed on board. Finally, at 11 a.m. on Tuesday 22 December 1915, *Britannic* slipped her moorings alongside a frosty Gladstone Dock and pulled out into the Mersey, only to promptly drop anchor and remain immobile for the rest of the day. The problem, however, was not serious, but simply due to the fact that 200 medical orderlies were still en route from Aldershot and were not liable to be on board until midnight. If nothing else, it gave those members of the medical staff who were already on board an ideal opportunity to explore and familiarise themselves with the ship, but the missing orderlies finally boarded just before midnight and within twenty minutes *Britannic* was finally headed out into the Irish Sea.

Britannic in Southampton Water. (TBF)

Britannic at Southampton, with the blue ensign of a RNR captain flying at the stern. (TBF)

4

THE MAIDEN VOYAGE

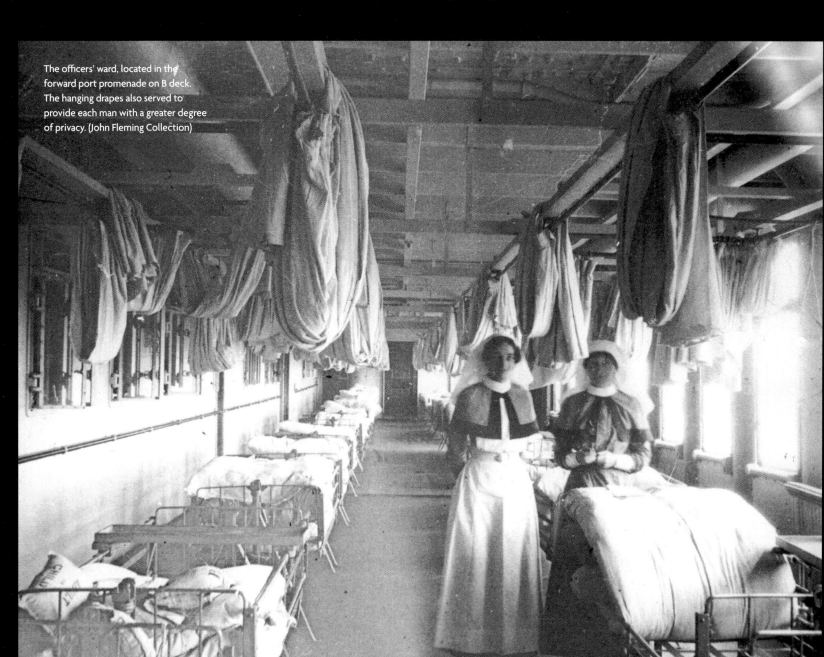

The officers' ward, located in the forward port promenade on B deck. The hanging drapes also served to provide each man with a greater degree of privacy. (John Fleming Collection)

In spite of the secrecy that surrounds activities on most military vessels, *Britannic*'s maiden voyage is surprisingly well documented, courtesy of the diary of Dr Harold Goodman, a 39-year-old medical doctor from Hemsworth in Yorkshire. In fact, Goodman had only been appointed as a lieutenant in the Royal Army Medical Corps (RAMC) on 14 December and his attachment to a hospital ship, generally seen as a less arduous posting, may well have been seen as a way of breaking him in gently.

Britannic's maiden voyage would have none of the glamour associated with those of her elder sisters, and, once the initial excitement had worn off, for the next nine days Goodman's diary would record an atmosphere of almost complete monotony:

23rd: R.A.M.C. men turned up at 12 midnight, ship left, destination unknown, to any of us. Rumour says Australia but probably all bunkum. Parade at 10.30 a.m. and Coln. Anderson [in command] made a round of the ship. Find from orders I am with Capt. Clark, Lieuts. Anderson, Pender, and Bachelor and allotted F, L, V, M, N wards, 426 beds on starboard forward part of ship on F and G decks. Two of our wards under water from leaks in porthole and back pressure from faulty valve in ship's tank which allows water to pump back through sink. Wards are two decker cots. Nearly everyone ill as strong squally southwest half gale blowing, so R.A.M.C. men do little. Spent a day doing very little but chat and shake down – very bored indeed. Had Cholera vacc. injected 5 p.m. ½cc.

24th: Same old gale, tables very thinly attended. Parade at 10.30. Coln. told us to carry on when he arrived which meant nothing doing for us. Lecture at 12 by Professor Squires and Mr. Risk of Belfast on virtues of urea as antiseptic: very interesting. Informed us that we should have six days only to treat wounded, so presume we go to Mudros in Mediterranean? News published and day's run put up, 426 nms done. Off Cape Finisterre at midday, so bound Gib. Had long chat with Mr. Risk and Dr. Rentril, both attached Belfast. Christmas eve, R.A.M.C. men recovering sporadically and handling matters.

Britannic could carry over 3,000 sick and wounded. These two photographs of F and D wards show that the accommodation for the other ranks was not quite so comfortable. D ward comprised single-tier cots, whereas the double-tiered cots in F ward were more representative of those on board a hospital ship. (Angus Mitchell Collection)

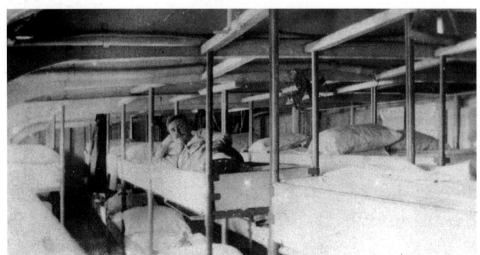

Christmas Day 25th: Boat rolled badly during night. Table overturned etc. not much sleep. Morning; heavy wind and squally. Service at 11 a.m. C of E. Saloon decorated with holly and mistletoe. After service, address by Coln. Anderson as to duties of embarkation and disembarkation. Our wards F, L, M, N, V, quite a simple matter as everything just forward of them although they are on E deck (forward) F (L. M. N.) G (V), a lift runs through middle of them. Day's run from 12 midday 24th to midday 25th is 443 miles. Cape St. Vincent we sighted at 2 p.m. and Sagres the signalling station. Saw here three tramps, first vessels we've sighted since just after we left (at 10.30 same morn.)

26th: Passed Gibraltar at 1.30 a.m., sighted the Spanish coast, Cape de Gata at 10 a.m. Life belt drill at 11.30 all hands and boat drill. African coast at 3 p.m., day's run to midday 455 miles.

27th: Day's run 416 miles, passed and sighted Sardinia. Concert in evening in R.A.M.C. mess.

28th: Passed Capri and entered bay of Naples at 8.30 a.m. On Capri Emperor Tiberius had a palace; ruins visible. Caves at foot, drop of 700 ft. into sea where Emperor Tiberius had a playful habit of dropping his victims to feed the lobsters. Hazy morning. Dropped anchor in Naples harbour and several went on shore

Although *Britannic*'s interiors were far from complete, this photograph of Lieutenant Urwick's B deck cabin shows a degree of comfort that many in the trenches would have envied. (Ronald Goodman Collection)

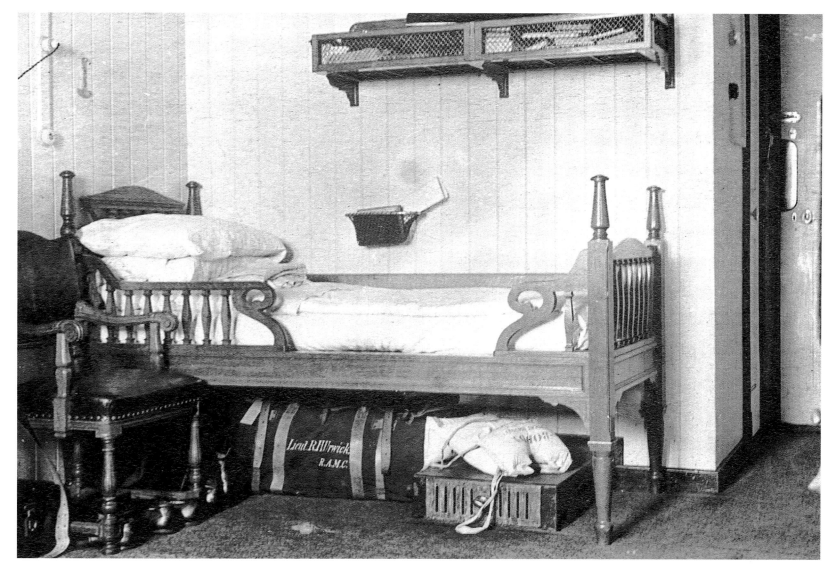

with passes. Spent rest of the day doing nothing and admiring the view. Passes issued at night. Coaling lighters alongside all day and coaling going on.

29th: Lectured orderlies from 8.45–9.30 in morn in wards which are getting straighter. Joined Urwick, Anderson and Bachelor and went on shore in motor launch landing at Arsenal step at 10.30am. Walked along through park to aquarium, thence to Cooks and changed notes, owing to prohibition of export of bullion, exchange on paper higher than in sterling. Walked up to Bertholmi lift and ascended to hotel where we lunched and drove down to quay and back on board at 2 p.m. Boat sailed at 4 slowly; beautiful view of Vesuvius, quite clear summit.

30th: Entered straights of Messina early morn, passing Stromboli about 5 a.m. Etna in sight at 7, remains of earthquake at Messina, ruined buildings visible as we came up. Scylla and Charybdis passed. Etna magnificently seen on Sicilian shore, apparently snow covered (10,000 ft.). Embarkation drill (Cranes and Cots) at 9 a.m.; busy in wards until 12.30. Steaming very fast after Messina straits passed, 20 knots at least. Lecture by Professor Squires [informal] at my request, on *Aeneid*, most interesting, in lounge at 9.30. Run up to 12 – 247 miles.

31st: First orderly duty, middle watch, 8–12 midday, 8–12 midnight. Accompanied Commander Dyke, Coln. Anderson and Captain Bartlett on round, went

The nurses enjoying a game of deck cricket along *Britannic's* aft promenade deck. The officer taking the photograph at the right seems to indicate that secrecy aboard a hospital ship was not an overriding concern, unlike on the Western Front, where the use of private cameras was not permitted. (John Fleming Collection)

through every ward on ship etc. time – 2 hours cont. travelling, most interesting. Passed in early morn and onwards during day the various islands, keeping Greece coast on port side, Passed Hagios Sprata island about 2 and arrived Lemnos at 4 p.m. Whole bay boomed and enormous quantity shipping of all descriptions in harbour. We anchored inside boom in 13 fathoms (78ft.) alongside 5 hospital ships, *Dunluce*, *Grantully Castle*, *Egypt*, and *Gloucester Castle* and *Assegai*. Monitor, old type, left harbour as we came. Whole aspect of Lemnos very hilly and looks utterly barren. Shore and slopes covered with tents and encampments. At 7 p.m. without any apparent warning the P&O *Assegai* and P&O *Egypt* came alongside and commenced discharging patients. The contrast in size of ships was extraordinary as their funnels only came up to our boat deck and seemed like lighters alongside. They discharged onto D deck by gangways from their decks which were about level. Very busy (and no dinner) until 11 p.m. Got our V ward (94) beds full and several in L and M and 10 in F ward. All these latter stretcher cases, the others walked and were helped on. Whole thing apparently not arranged for and certainly should have been left until morning. Coln. A and Capt. I believe, both on shore and therefore this arrangement probably not in accordance with their ideas but we shall know tomorrow. Bed about 2 a.m. after seeing New Year in, and may it end differently. All our patients got chicken broth or cocoa about 10 p.m. and settled for night.

New Year's Day, however, was to prove little different to the last day of 1915. Throughout the morning the

Medical staff relaxing on *Britannic*'s promenade deck. The fact that the nurses are wearing their capes and hats would suggest that they have either just arrived on board or are waiting to go ashore. (John Fleming Collection)

Three medical officers relaxing in standard White Star deck chairs beneath the davits on the aft port boat deck. This station included one of *Britannic*'s two motorboats, which were incorporated into the ship's complement of boats following the *Titanic* disaster. Each motorboat had its own wireless capability, although experience would show that the motorboat's engines were not always reliable. (Ronald Goodman Collection)

patients continued to come aboard from the *Egypt* and *Assegai*, with the hospital ships *Asturias* and *Killman Castle* alongside the following day. In addition, another 1,000 wounded had arrived on board via barges from the hospitals on shore, and there was no let-up into the evening when yet another convoy of barges arrived alongside carrying a batch of wounded officers.

For the patients, the sheer scale of *Britannic* was almost overwhelming. Private R.E. Atkinson of the 29th Divisional Cyclist Company had arrived at Mudros from Cairo on board the *Dunluce Castle* after being evacuated from Suvla Bay. Atkinson clearly recalled *Dunluce Castle* arriving alongside *Britannic* with a heavy thud, protected by large bundles of wood hanging alongside, before he boarded the larger ship from *Dunluce*'s well deck. Even then he clearly remembered having to go up another five decks before reaching *Britannic*'s boat deck, from where the *Dunluce Castle* looked no bigger than a trawler. Mesmerised from looking down into the engine room, seeing the telephones, lifts and swimming baths, Atkinson likened the ship to a town holding 6,000 patients. Within four hours he had been placed in H ward and had been 'marked up' as suffering with pleurisy by his allocated doctor; after that he was issued with his blue hospital suit and given a good dinner.

Unfortunately, from here on in it was all downhill and the following day's entry in Atkinson's diary seemed to indicate a definite turn for the worse:

> Grub is rotten, starvation, two slices for breakfast, dinner, stew in a basin, thought it was soup first course, but nothing else came up. Patients get nearly frozen waiting to get on from trawlers, some stretcher cases get douched with water from ship's side. Cocoa and hard biscuit for supper. Church in evening, gilt edge prayer books W.S.L. Cocoa and biscuits for supper.

Meanwhile, the last of the injured continued to come aboard. By the morning of 3 January the last of the wounded officers had arrived from ashore and at 3 p.m., after landing the body of Private Arthur Howe of the 1st/5th Essex Regiment, who had died the previous day from tubercular disease, the fully loaded *Britannic* slipped through the defensive boom of Mudros Harbour and headed at full speed toward the south-west. By 9 p.m. the ship had clocked up 120 miles and was north of Andros, with a clear run ahead for the Kea Channel. Harold Goodman recollected a lovely evening sitting out on deck until 10 p.m., but for poor old Private Atkinson languishing in the bowels of H ward it was a basic supper consisting of cocoa and hard biscuits, followed by a single Lills cigarette.

The homeward journey would be very different to the more leisurely atmosphere on the voyage out. Instead of the empty wards, the ship was now full of injured or convalescent soldiers and Captain Bartlett was still

obliged to carry out the lifeboat drill. Having said that, *Britannic*'s odds for survival were now getting better by the minute. The daily run to midday on 4 January was 430 miles and, when the ship passed Malta shortly before midnight, the passage into the western Mediterranean signified that the ship had successfully completed the most hazardous stage of the journey.

But it was not to be. Life on a passenger steamer is rarely predictable, less so on a serving hospital ship in a war zone, but no one could have foreseen the sudden cry of 'man overboard!' shortly after 6.30 a.m. on 5 January. In normal circumstances the captain's first option would have been to stop the ship, but the rules on one of

A group of medical officers on the boat deck. This area of the ship was reserved for the ship's officers and medical staff only. The riveted structure immediately behind the group housed one of the motors that would enable the larger davits to be operated. (Ronald Goodman Collection)

Programme of Concert

Held on Board

HOSPITAL SHIP "BRITANNIC,"

TUESDAY EVENING, FEBRUARY 8th, 1916,

Under the Patronage of

Capt. C. A. BARTLETT, C.B., and Lieut.-Col. H. S. ANDERSON

— PROGRAMME —

Opening Chorus, " Are we all here, yes"	The " Dug Ups"
Cornet Solo, Selected	Trumpet-Major Geary
Serio Comic, Selected	Driver Marshall
Song, Selected	Corporal Hutchings
Comic Song, "Bobbing Down"	Private Kemp
Selected	Lieutenant Crawford
Song, Selected	C.S.M. Hogan
Pianoforte Solo, Selected	Private Soothill
Phonofiddleoddities	P.O. Pilkington

— INTERVAL —

Night Operations	Capt. Adams and Lieuts Crawford & Vines
Comic Song, Selected	Lieutenant Vernon
Song, Selected	Corporal Hutchings
Song, Selected	Lieutenant Feddon
Recitation, Selected	Captain Morrow
Song, " Nipper's Lullaby"	Captain Wingate
" Whistling Chorus"	Private Stockley
Song, Selected	Private Lever
Humorous, Selected	Private Templeton

THE KING.

To break the monotony of the outward journey, on-board concerts would often be held to keep up the troops' morale. (Author)

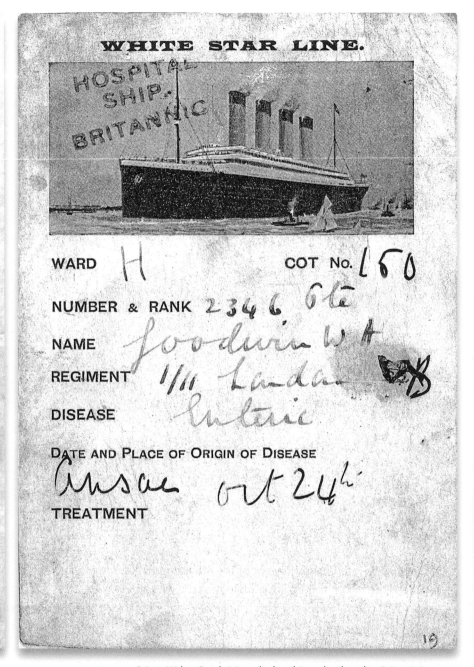

Private Walter Goodwin's medical card, issued on boarding *Britannic* in January 1916. Aside from the customary regimental information, the cards also contained information of a patient's illness and, when necessary, information regarding any specific treatment or diet. (Author)

His Majesty's transports when in a war zone were very different. There was no going back; all that could be done was to search the ship to see if everyone was accounted for. By the end of the morning the medical staff had finished searching their wards and it was discovered that a naval rating named Samuel Jones, of the Drake Battalion, Royal Naval Division, was indeed missing. In accordance with the established military procedures, at 3 p.m. a formal court of inquiry was held on board to ascertain how and why Jones had gone overboard, but with no evidence one way or the other to indicate why. In the end the ship's log simply recorded: 'It is reasonable to assume that he is dead.'

As *Britannic* continued to head west, hugging the African coast for most of what was to be a fine, warm morning and a hot sunny afternoon, the only bad news seemed to be that Private Atkinson was involved in yet another row with the stewards about the scarce food. Gibraltar was passed at 10 p.m. the following evening and, once into the Atlantic, *Britannic* continued to work up to speed, clocking up no less than 506 miles in the twenty-four-hour period up to midday on 7 January. Twenty-four hours and another 512 miles later, *Britannic* was off Cape Finisterre, where the patients were each issued with another six cigarettes, and by the evening of 8 January the ship was safely through Biscay and approaching the French island of Ushant, where they passed the empty and outward-bound *Mauretania*. Home was now less than a day away and, as if to confirm their imminent arrival, that night the patients had their khaki uniforms returned in preparation for disembarkation the following morning.

For *Britannic*'s medical staff, Sunday 9 January was going to be a long day. The morning started particularly badly when Private Charles Vincent of the 8th Hampshire Regiment died from tuberculosis while the ship was off the Cornish coast. However, although normal procedure would have been to carry out a burial at sea within a day, as *Britannic* was so close to home the decision was taken instead to place the body in the ship's mortuary. Later that morning, *Britannic* was off the Isle of Wight where, observed by a hydroplane and with two minesweepers leading the way, the ship was guided through the buoyed channel that led into the Solent, where two more patrol boats took over the escort duties. *Britannic* slowly edged her way up the misty Solent and into Southampton Water. For those on deck there were at least some distractions, especially when one of the five aeroplanes that were scouting on the Portsmouth side flew over the ship and exchanged salutes.

If nothing else, the slow progress meant that there was still time for the patients to scribble a last-minute letter home, and making the most of his unexpected opportunity, Private Walter Alexander Goodwin, a typhoid patient in H ward, took the chance to send a note to his father in Hackney:

Britannic
9th January 1916.

Dear Dad,
    Just a line to let you know that I am within a few miles of England. I left Port Said on the 26th Dec. and travelled to Alexandria by train, and then embarked on the H/S Dunluce Castle, which sailed that night for Mudros bay, the naval base of the Eastern Front, we waited there for two days for the above hospital ship, a magnificent boat of 50,000 tons larger than the Aquitania, this is her maiden voyage, so you see I have the privilege of saying that I am one of the first passengers to sail on the sister-ship of the Titanic.
    We have had a splendid voyage, so smooth has been the passage, that one would scarcely realise that you were afloat. Rumour has it that the choleric patients are going to Croydon. Will write again as soon as I arrive at my destination.
I remain
Your affectionate son,
Wallie

Progress along Southampton Water was a little quicker, but in spite of the congestion it was still possible to see the towering funnels of *Aquitania* from some way off as she lay in the White Star Dock. Ever so slowly, the six escorting tugs, three forward and three aft, manoeuvred *Britannic* into the dock, but it would not be until three o'clock that the first of the 4,200 invalids finally began to disembark, at the beginning of a process that would take a further eight hours before Harold Goodman would see the last of his patients ashore. The work would go on until eleven o'clock that night and it would be well past midnight before Goodman finally got to bed, but even then it would not be for long, as he was due back in his ward at 4 a.m. Fortunately, the following day would not be such an arduous one and, after obtaining a pass until Sunday 16 January, he was soon en route to Guildford, where he would spend the first part of his six-day leave.

As for the patients, they were dispatched to numerous medical facilities across the country. Unfortunately, for Walter Goodwin the rumours of him being sent to Croydon were no more than that, and instead he found himself an inmate of the Third West General Hospital at Ninian Park, Cardiff – over 100 miles from his home in north-east London. For Private Atkinson, however, it looked as if his luck had finally turned. After getting ashore his ambulance train departed from Southampton at 7 p.m.; it would still not reach Waterloo for another four hours, but once there he found hundreds of gentlemen's fine motorcars waiting to transport the patients to their hospitals. Atkinson's vehicle would take him to the Southwark Military Hospital, better known during peacetime as the Camberwell Infirmary, in Dulwich, and his diary for Monday 10 January 1916 ends on what would seem, for once, to be a happier note: 'Inspected by doctor, no sign of T.B. Comfortable ward, plenty of food, extra for breakfast.'

5

BRITANNIC'S WAR

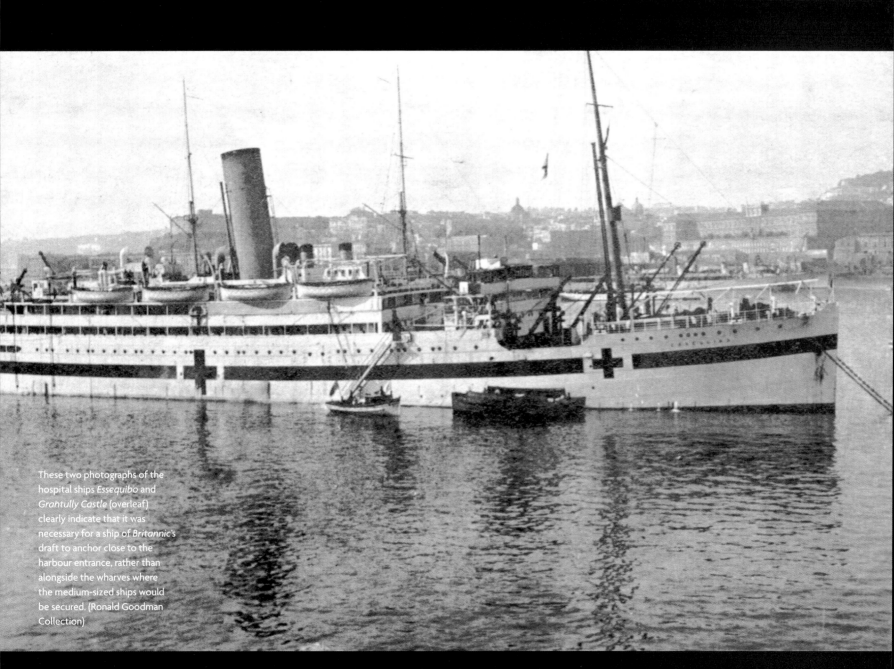

These two photographs of the hospital ships *Essequibo* and *Grantully Castle* (overleaf) clearly indicate that it was necessary for a ship of *Britannic*'s draft to anchor close to the harbour entrance, rather than alongside the wharves where the medium-sized ships would be secured. (Ronald Goodman Collection)

After only eleven days in port *Britannic* was once again outward bound for the Mediterranean, but by this time, unlike the excitement of the first voyage, the routine on board had settled down into its customary mundane military drudgery. For the nurses this would mean plenty of bed making, which the matron fully expected to be complete by the time the ship reached Naples. This would become the established staging post for the outward journey.

On her second voyage *Britannic* would arrive at Naples at 7 a.m. on 25 January, and throughout the day would take on 2,510 tons of coal and another 1,500 tons of fresh water. The intention was to sail at first light in order to arrive at Mudros at dawn on the morning of 28 January, but as the medical staff were settling down for the evening a telegram arrived from the principal naval transport officer at Cairo, instructing Captain Bartlett to remain at Naples and take on wounded patients from the hospital ship *Grantully Castle*, which had been redirected while en route for Mudros.

In the end, *Britannic*'s voyage to Mudros would never be completed and the ship would remain at Naples for eleven days. *Grantully Castle* duly arrived alongside on 27 February and that afternoon, during a three-hour

period, transferred 438 patients aboard *Britannic*. Barely an hour after *Grantully Castle* had completed her transfer of invalids, the hospital ship *Formosa* also began to transfer even more patients aboard *Britannic*; by 8.40 p.m. a further 393 wounded had been taken on board. There then followed three days of uncertainty before further orders were received, instructing *Britannic* to await the arrival of the hospital ships *Essequibo*, *Nevasa* and *Panama*, before returning to England. For the senior medical staff this meant a relatively relaxed few days, giving Harold Goodman and his colleagues a welcome opportunity to go ashore for excursions to Pompeii and the museums, or, for those who preferred to go ashore during the evening, trips to the opera to see Verdi's *Otello*, Puccini's *Tosca* and even the comic ballet *Coppelia*.

For the ship's crew, however, the routine continued uninterrupted. On 26 January the American cruiser USS *Des Moines* had arrived in port, and the British Consul at Naples had taken the opportunity to instruct Captain Bartlett and Lieutenant Colonel Anderson to invite the American captain aboard to inspect the ship. As luck would have it, two days later the American Ambassador to Italy, Nelson Page, also happened to be in Naples holidaying with his wife and daughter. They too were invited aboard the ship to have a look around, the British consular authorities no doubt welcoming the opportunity to have the ship inspected by the representative of a neutral power who could provide independent confirmation that *Britannic* was unarmed and everything that she claimed to be.

Essequibo finally arrived alongside early on the morning of 1 February and began transferring her 594 wounded, the procedure closely observed by a representative from the local Italian sanitary authority. Twenty-four hours later the hospital ship *Nevasa*, carrying another 493 patients, was also alongside, but it would not be until the morning of 4 February that the transfer of the remaining 319 invalids from *Panama* could commence. However, the final transfer was completed within three hours and *Britannic* was finally westbound and headed for home by 3.15 p.m., arriving back at Southampton early on the afternoon of 9 February.

From an operational point of view the use of Naples for the transfer of the patients had been a success, but the Neapolitan Sanitary Authorities, wary of the potential dangers of infection at the port, not to mention the possibility of upsetting their former German and Austro-Hungarian allies, had raised objections to any further use of the port for medical transfers. The neutral Italians still agreed to allow Allied vessels to take on coal and water at the port, but suggested that from now on if the British were to make any use of an Italian port for transferring patients then the Sicilian port of Augusta would be more appropriate. This port had its disadvantages, not least the lack of jetties and the open anchorage, which could be very exposed with a south-easterly wind. But with the Dardanelles having already been evacuated and the number of casualties having dropped significantly, the Admiralty Transport Division felt that the option would be worth exploring.

When *Britannic* next departed from Southampton at 1 p.m. on 22 February it would be a very short trip. In fact, the ship was only being moved in order to vacate her badly needed berth in the White Star Dock, and *Britannic* would remain anchored off Cowes for almost a month before finally departing on her third voyage to the Mediterranean on 20 March 1916. As before, there was no inkling of the final destination, although by now the medical staff were reasonably confident that it would be Naples, where indeed the ship duly arrived five days later. After taking on coal and water as usual, *Britannic* arrived at Augusta on 28 March.

Two shots of HMHS *Britannic*, taken in the bright Mediterranean sun at Naples on 8 February 1916, on her second voyage. The photographs show *Britannic*'s still gleaming paintwork at its best, with hardly a blemish to be seen. The stern shot overleaf clearly shows the patients in their medical suits, along with one of the ship's boy scouts serving as a messenger on the docking bridge. (Michail Michailakis/Mark Chirnside Collection)

The day would be a busy one, with the hospital ships *Dunluce Castle*, *Egypt* and *Glengorm Castle* all transferring their patients throughout the day, while the hospital ship *Valdivia* transferred a number of patients and also part of a Canadian field hospital unit by barge. The work continued throughout the next day, affording Captain Bartlett an opportunity to send a landing party ashore to collect some sand in order to clean the ship's wooden decks – he wasn't known as 'Holystone Charlie' by his crews for nothing. At 9 a.m. the following morning the hospital ship *Formosa* had also arrived alongside carrying both patients and men of the 1st London Field Hospital, who were travelling back to England; by 3 p.m. the transfer was complete and *Britannic* was once again headed for home, arriving safely back at Southampton at 11 a.m. on 4 April.

Britannic's future employment, however, was uncertain by this time. The unexpected Gallipoli evacuation had, for the time being at least, massively reduced the number of casualties from the eastern Mediterranean theatre of war, to the point where the larger liners were suddenly no longer required. *Mauretania* had been released from service on 1 March, followed six weeks later by *Aquitania* on 10 April, and on the afternoon of 11 April, *Britannic* once again departed from the White Star Dock; for the foreseeable future she was to remain anchored in the Solent off Cowes at half-rate (5s per gross ton) until the Transport Division could make a decision on their last giant hospital ship. Pressure from the cash-strapped War Office finally persuaded them that they could no longer afford to keep the ship in service and on 21 May the crew was finally paid off; the White Star Line was advanced £76,000 in order to cover the cost of reinstating the ship to commercial service and two weeks later *Britannic* was officially released from government service.

After barely five months in service and having completed only three voyages, *Britannic* was once again surplus to requirement. With the Mediterranean reasonably subdued there was little chance that the ship would be required in the short term, and it was not until the opening of a new German offensive in the Balkans in August 1916, followed by an Allied counter-attack in September, that this picture would change. On 28 August, the White Star Line was once again informed that *Britannic* was required for government service.

The hierarchy on board remained unaltered. Captain Bartlett was reappointed to command on 4 September, allowing him almost three weeks to prepare his ship, but for the medical staff it was much more of a last-minute arrangement. Ms Elizabeth Anne Dowse, the ship's new matron, would only arrive at Southampton to assume her post on 22 September, while Lieutenant Colonel Anderson would only be reappointed to his old command twenty-four hours before *Britannic* was scheduled to depart. However, by 5.40 p.m. on 24 September, the medical orderlies were aboard, albeit in a state of virtual chaos, and *Britannic* was once again outward bound for Mudros via Naples, arriving at her destination on 3 October. After two days the transfer of wounded was completed and *Britannic* departed for Southampton on a voyage that was largely uneventful, save for the death of Corporal Joseph Seddon of the 1st Battalion Manchester Regiment, who died shortly after departing from Mudros and was buried at sea later that night.

Britannic departing from Naples on 8 February 1916, with Vesuvius clearly visible in the background. (Michail Michailakis/Mark Chirnside Collection)

Up until this point *Britannic*'s period of service had been relatively straightforward, but controversy would surround her fifth voyage and, to a certain extent, this controversy remains responsible for the shadow of doubt that lingers over the ship to this day.

On 17 October 1916, the Admiralty had approved a request by the RAMC to transport stores and medical personnel as passengers on *Britannic*; when the ship departed as scheduled on 20 October, along with her official complement of medical staff, she also had on board an additional 483 medical personnel and 2,762 packages of medical stores bound for theatres of war in Egypt, Malta, Salonika, India and Mesopotamia. The extra personnel were all non-combatants and the transport of medical supplies was hardly a matter that could be regarded as illegal for a hospital ship, but subsequent observations of these activities would cause no end of problems in the coming months.

Britannic arrived at Mudros at 8 a.m. on 28 October and over the next two days she would take on board 3,022 casualties from the hospital ships *Dunluce Castle*, *Glenart Castle*, *Llandovery Castle*, *Grantully Castle* and *Valdivia*. At the same time, the medical personnel who had been brought out from England would be transferred to these vessels for transportation to their ultimate postings.

Another of these ships, *Wandilla*, had recently arrived from Malta and amongst the invalids carried in this ship was one Adalbert Franz Messany, a 24-year-old Austrian opera singer who had been in Egypt when the war broke out. Initially he had been interned on Malta and, having

Britannic at Mudros, taking on wounded from two smaller hospital ships at the same time. (Alasdair Fairbairn Collection)

fallen ill with tuberculosis, he was now being repatriated to Austria via neutral Holland; but, on witnessing the transfer of the uniformed medical personnel and packages from *Britannic*, along with his observations and claims of British officers retaining their side arms during the passage home, it provided the Central Powers with a golden propaganda opportunity. When the German Government published a document on 29 January 1917 listing twenty-two cases of alleged Allied abuses in the use and operation of hospital ships, *Britannic* was one of the vessels cited in its pages, and it is no coincidence that two days later Germany resumed its campaign of unrestricted submarine warfare.

In the meantime, *Britannic* duly departed from Mudros shortly after midday on 30 October and during the voyage to Southampton Messany, with surprisingly few restrictions, was able to speak freely with a number of his fellow passengers. Included in this number were two soldiers, Harold Hickman and Reginald Taplay, both of whom, he would later state, claimed to be translators being transferred to France. Somehow Messany came to believe that there were also 2,500 men on board who had been ordered to stay below decks and were being fed different food from the hospital patients. To further complicate matters, when the ship reached Southampton on 6 November, Messany even observed these men marching away in military formation, although he did admit that they were not actually carrying any weapons.

Messany's allegations – indeed the entire German document – obliged the Admiralty to counter all the accusations in great detail, and every effort was made to trace the two soldiers mentioned in the document. However, while Messany's references to their being translators were true, if only to a certain extent, for the most part the remainder of his allegations clearly lacked any real substance. It eventually transpired that Private Reginald Taplay was a soldier in the RAMC who was suffering from dysentery, while Private Harold Hickman, of the Welsh Hussars, was being sent home following an attack of malaria. Both denied ever claiming to be interpreters, although it was true that because they could both speak a foreign language their uniforms had

Approaching *Britannic* – taken from the hospital ship *Dunluce Castle*. (Alasdair Fairbairn Collection)

Britannic at Mudros with an unidentified hospital ship alongside. (Michail Michailakis/ Mark Chirnside Collection)

an 'L' on the sleeves. This was not unusual; in fact, it was a distinguishing feature that any soldier on the Salonika front with a foreign language would carry on his uniform.

As for the 2,500 men who were allegedly ordered to remain out of sight and marched away after the ship arrived in Southampton, a breakdown of the 3,022 invalids on board during the voyage revealed that only 367 were actually what would be referred to as 'cot cases', and therefore unable to leave their beds. The walking wounded would certainly have been on different rations to those of the more seriously ill patients on board, whose prescribed diets would have varied from patient to patient. As to their being confined below decks, the point was made that there were absolutely no restrictions on any of the men being allowed to go top side, just so long as they were permitted by the senior medical officer and provided they wore their blue hospital suits.

Above: Looking up from the decks of the *Dunluce Castle*, secured along *Britannic*'s starboard side. (Alasdair Fairbairn Collection)

Britannic at Mudros in October 1916. The additional motor house on the aft shade deck was installed before the ship was recalled for government service. (TBF)

There was one accusation, however, that did seem to be a palpable hit, concerning the fact that the officers had been allowed to retain side arms which were their personal property. The British claimed that the conveyance of weapons belonging to wounded officers was not thought to be in contravention of the Hague Convention, but while it may have been a relatively minor breach of the regulations, it had become something of a grey area and was undoubtedly enough to blur the line between what was or was not permitted.

Ultimately Messany's allegations would not have any impact on *Britannic*'s eventual fate, as he was not repatriated until some weeks after the ship had been lost, but even so the whole affair could have been seen as embarrassing to the Admiralty. Following *Britannic*'s loss, the British newspapers had been quick to accuse Germany of every seagoing atrocity that they could imagine. However, if the German Government could not justify the sinking of a hospital ship in human terms, the allegations that *Britannic* was not entirely what she claimed to be could certainly muddy the waters and help them in terms of damage limitation.

A lesser-known view of *Britannic* taken from the port quarter. By October 1916 the ship's once gleaming white paintwork was beginning to look decidedly shabby, but with resources stretched to the limit the paintwork on a transport vessel was not considered to be a top priority. (Bruce Beveridge Collection)

Valdivia secured alongside *Britannic* in October 1916. (TBF)

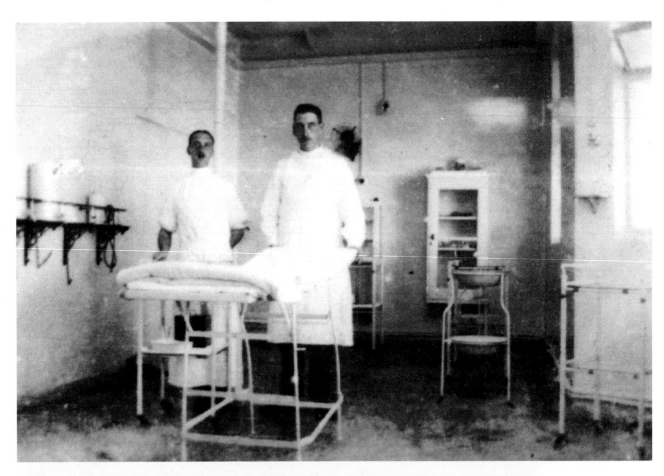

A rare internal photograph of the medical facilities. (Alasdair Fairbairn Collection)

A rare *Britannic* artefact: the keys to the cooling room of the ship's Turkish bath, which during the war was used to store the invalids' military uniforms while they were on board. (Author)

Capable of carrying thirty-four mines, *U73* was larger than the preceding class of UC coastal minelayers. With an operational range of 7,500 nautical miles, in April 1916 the U-boat was bound for the Mediterranean, arriving at the port of Cattaro after a cruise of thirty days. Due to the hardships of the voyage, it would be three months before she was ready for her next mine-laying operations off Salonika and Mudros. (TBF)

Britannic's final visit to Southampton lasted less than a week. With *Aquitania* undergoing repairs after a heavy storm and the medical authorities at Mudros urgently requesting another large hospital ship to be sent out from England to evacuate even more wounded, *Britannic* left Southampton in the early afternoon of 12 November in her fastest turnaround to date.

It was a calm if bitterly cold Sunday afternoon, but the ship made steady progress, passing through the Straits of Gibraltar around midnight on the 15th and arriving at Naples on the morning of 17 November to take on coal and water as usual. *Britannic* was actually ready for sea that same afternoon, but when a heavy storm blew up Captain Bartlett had little option but to remain in harbour and ride it out. According to Rev. John Fleming, *Britannic*'s Presbyterian chaplain, the ship was actually secured by her three bow anchors and twenty hawsers fastening her stern to the wharf, and yet even then she was in danger. By the afternoon of Sunday 19 November the weather cleared just long enough for Captain Bartlett to take the opportunity to put to sea, but the respite did not last long and once again the sea began to rise shortly after the ship had cleared the harbour. By the following morning,

Right: Rev. John Alexander Fleming was one of the first Presbyterian ministers to serve in a hospital ship, sharing the workload with the Church of England chaplain, Rev. James Atkinson. Based in Stepps (Glasgow) at the outbreak of war, Fleming joined the Army Chaplains Department. After serving in Scotland, Fleming was appointed to *Britannic* in September 1916 and would go on to write and publish the only contemporary account of life on the hospital ship. (John Fleming Collection)

Below: The log of the destroyer HMS *Rattlesnake* clearly recorded the loss of the French transport *Burdigala* to a torpedo, allowing a crucial clue that may have saved *Britannic* to go un-investigated. (National Archives)

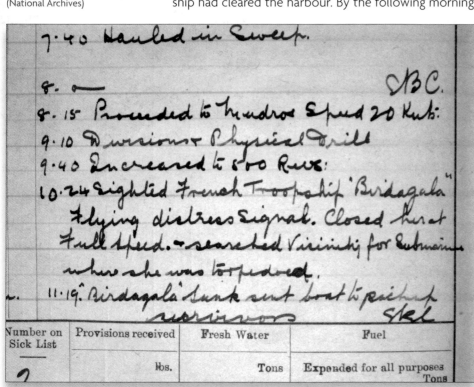

however, *Britannic* had passed through the Straits of Messina and the Mediterranean was once again looking its best.

As the ship raced eastwards toward the Aegean Sea one of the great twists of fate in her story becomes apparent. *Britannic* had last arrived at Mudros on 28 October, on the same day that the German mine-laying submarine *U73* had been active in the Gulf of Athens. In fact, it is entirely possible that when Kapitänleutnant Gustav Siess, *U73*'s commanding officer, wrote in his log on the evening of 27 October and again at 3.25 a.m. the following morning that he had sighted hospital ships in the Kea Channel, that *Britannic* may well have been one of them. Later that day Siess had even taken up a firing position on another vessel, only for the attack to be aborted at the very last minute when he realised that he had in fact been stalking a hospital ship. Within hours of *Britannic* passing through the Kea Channel that day, *U73* had laid two mine barriers, each consisting of six mines, on the Kea side of the strait, and even though *Britannic* had safely avoided

3h50Vm.	Petalioi - Golf	Jm Golf ein Zerstörer in Sicht;in der Keos-Strasse mit S-Kurs ein Lazarettschiff.
5h10Vm.		Bei Hellwerden getaucht und auf Platz für Minenwerfen gesteuert.Die Dampfer fahren alle auf der Keos-Seite der Strasse. Nach Hellwerden sind viele Dampfer in Sicht.
8h07Vm bis 8h27Vm		Zwei Sperren zu je 6 Minen geworfen. (s.Sperrmeldung).

being damaged on her return journey, by the morning of Tuesday 21 November she was making a healthy 20 knots and was once again headed straight for the danger zone.

Although everything seemed under control, without realising it Captain Bartlett actually had every reason to be concerned. Exactly one week earlier the 12,481grt French troopship *Burdigala*, while en route from Salonika to Toulon, had struck one of *U73*'s mines in the Kea Channel. On that occasion the British destroyer HMS *Rattlesnake* had been nearby and was able to assist before *Burdigala* slipped beneath the surface at 11.19 a.m., but by 12.30 p.m. *Rattlesnake* had picked up all of the 380 survivors and was en route to Piraeus.

It is here that another of the great 'ifs' in *Britannic*'s story comes into play. *Rattlesnake*'s log clearly records that the *Burdigala* had been torpedoed, this observation no doubt based on the statements and reports of the French steamer's captain and crew. To further strengthen the U-boat claim, one of *Burdigala*'s guns had reported firing on a periscope, but while the French gun crew may well have believed that they had seen a periscope, this particular red herring was to have disastrous consequences for *Britannic*. If it had not been for the false U-boat report then it is practically certain that after *Burdigala*'s loss a wider stretch of the Kea Channel would have been swept, even though it was originally considered to be too deep for mines. Instead, a vital clue went unnoticed and eleven mines continued to lurk beneath the surface, just deep enough to claim one of the larger battleships or transports that would sooner or later pass that way.

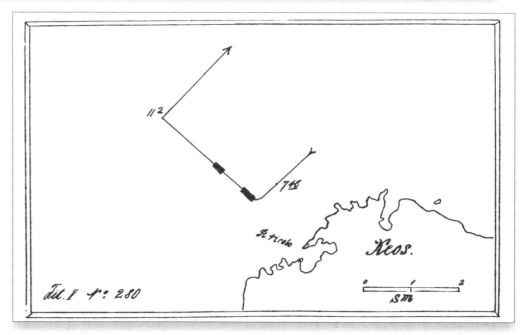

The war diary and map of *U73* provides detailed information on mine barrier thirty-two, laid in the Kea Channel on 28 October 1916. The twelve-mine barrier was intentionally laid on the Kea side of the strait, deep enough so that it would claim a larger transport rather than one of the many smaller vessels that travelled through the Kea Channel on a daily basis. (TBF)

Shortly before 8 a.m., while off Angalistros Point on the island of Makronisos, Captain Bartlett altered course to N48°E in order to bring the ship into the Kea Channel. Chief Officer Robert Hume and Fourth Officer David McTavish were the officers on watch up on the bridge, and as eight bells were sounded Seaman J. Murray took over from George Honeycott as lookout in the crow's nest. Considering the fact that it was a bright and sunny morning with a calm, glass-like sea, he would probably have been looking forward to a reasonably uneventful period on watch.

In the lounge the nurses were equally unconcerned, just sitting down to what would probably be their last meal before the ship was due to arrive at Mudros. With

67

The standard German contact mine carried an explosive charge of 150kg. *U73* carried thirty-four of these mines, with all three of the barriers laid in October 1916, accounting for two ships sunk, two damaged and amounting to a total of 71,227grt. (Author)

slightly more on her mind, Stewardess Violet Jessop – a lady who had not only survived the loss of *Titanic*, but had also been on board *Olympic* in September 1911 during her collision with the armoured cruiser HMS *Hawke* – was busy making up a breakfast tray for one of the nurses who was lying ill in her cabin, while Nurse Sheila Macbeth was rushing into the dining room late for breakfast. Rev. Fleming, also late for breakfast, hadn't even left his cabin and was casually gazing out of his porthole at the distant island.

On the surface everything seemed completely normal, when at 8.12 a.m. the apparent calm was shattered by the sound of a loud explosion, which Fleming later described as '... if a score of plate glass windows had been smashed together'. Sheila Macbeth also remembered feeling a great shudder run along the entire length of the ship, as did 15-year-old scout George Perman, who was on duty and operating one of the ship's lifts further aft. When interviewed eighty-three years after the disaster, Perman could still remember the impact as if it were yesterday: 'When the thing struck us, or we struck it, the whole ship shuddered. That was my first recognition that something had happened. Oh she absolutely shuddered, and immediately the cry went round: "The ship is sinking!"'

Up in the ship's lounge, Major Harold Priestly of the RAMC quickly took command of the situation. A veteran of the retreat from Mons and after eighteen months as a prisoner of war at Wittenberg, followed by nine months recovering from pleurisy, Priestley had been posted to *Britannic* on 2 November and was only nine days into his first voyage. The commotion had startled many of the nurses at their breakfast but, taking control of the situation, Priestley simply stood up and instructed the nurses to continue with their meal as the emergency alarm had not been sounded.

It was not long in coming. Following the crash, Rev. Fleming found himself with just enough time to check his allocated ward below to make sure that no one was in need of assistance before the alarm began to sound and within seconds the eerie calm aboard the ship was transformed. Nurse Ada Garland clearly remembered hearing the instruction: 'Ladies go to your cabins, put on your life-belts and go up to the boat deck!' The order did not need to be repeated, as the nurses immediately filed

Violet Jessop was more than familiar with the Olympic-class liners, having served as a stewardess on *Olympic*, *Titanic* and *Britannic*. In later life she declared that her escape from *Britannic* was the worst experience of her career, during which she sustained a gash in her thigh and what would later be identified as a cracked skull. (Margaret & Mary Meehan Collection)

Through her diary, Sheila Macbeth became one of *Britannic*'s best-known nurses. Enlisting in the QAIMNS in 1915, she was posted to *Britannic* in September 1916 and would later return to the ship sixty years after her loss at the invitation of Jacques Cousteau. (Angus Mitchell Collection)

out of the room, heading for their cabins. Sheila Macbeth also remembered to take her pillow, eiderdown and a coat, as well as her Gieve waistcoat – a personal flotation device similar to a rubber ring – before going up on deck. Perhaps not surprisingly for Rev. Fleming, the priority was to fetch his coat and Bible, before once again heading for the relative security of the boat deck.

Below decks, medical orderly Private Percy Tyler told of a far less dramatic reaction to the explosion. Sitting on his bunk in Barrack Room 2, aft on G deck, he was industriously polishing his tunic buttons when he recalled feeling a violent bump which 'sent me forward a few paces and back again, then the boat regularly danced'. As with the reaction to *Titanic*'s collision with the iceberg, no one really seemed to take very much notice; some of the men made casual remarks about having hit something, while others said that they were sorry for the boat they had run into. However, when another orderly ran in a few minutes later to say that the alarm had sounded and that the captain had ordered everyone to go up on deck with their lifebelts, the apparent lack of concern quickly evaporated.

For a few less fortunate individuals the consequences of the explosion were far more immediate. One of the ship's medical orderlies in the forward lavatory on E deck was nearly overwhelmed by the flow of water as it came up the hatch like a huge wave. Stumbling aft through the wreckage and debris towards the main staircase, he just managed to get through the watertight door before it closed behind him. Private John Cuthbertson was even more fortunate: alone in the forward barrack room on G deck, he was completely swept away by a massive inrush of water and, although the staircase had been destroyed in the blast, he eventually found himself washed up as far as E deck before he was finally able to extricate himself.

Up on the bridge, Captain Bartlett was also only too aware of the situation. Rising from his breakfast, his sudden presence on the bridge, even though still dressed in his pyjamas, was enough to reassure James Vickers, a 15-year-old scout who only moments before had been standing in the wheelhouse contemplating nothing more taxing than having his own breakfast. He later recalled: 'My heart was in my mouth, but when I saw the captain standing there, cool and quiet, I thought to myself it's all right, and felt a good deal more comfortable.'

Captain Bartlett's cool and quiet exterior, however, did not betray the true seriousness of the situation. Orders were immediately given to stop the ship's engines, close the watertight doors and to clear away the boats, but within minutes the damage reports began to arrive on the bridge. As the tally of bad news mounted, so *Britannic*'s chances of survival began to look increasingly grim.

A massive explosion had occurred on the ship's starboard side in the vicinity of bulkhead no. 3, but although only two compartments were open to the sea, which was comfortably within *Britannic*'s safety margin, the reality of the situation was far worse. The ship's watertight skin only extended as far forward as Boiler Room 6 and the blast had not only destroyed the bulkhead between Holds 2 and 3, but it had also damaged the bulkhead between Hold 1 and the forepeak.

In theory, *Britannic* should have been able to float with anything up to six of her forward compartments flooded, but although only four were actually open to the sea, there was worse news to come. The forward firemen's passage had also been damaged by the blast and for reasons unknown the watertight doors between Hold 3 and Boiler Room 6 had failed to close. With the watertight door between Boiler Rooms 6 and 5 also failing to close properly, within a couple of minutes both of these compartments had been evacuated, leaving *Britannic* perilously close to her designed safety threshold.

With *Britannic*'s situation deteriorating rapidly, Captain Bartlett ordered the remaining watertight doors closed and a distress signal to be sent, signalling that the ship had struck a mine off Port St Nikolo. At the same time the crew were ordered to uncover and lower the lifeboats over the side, although the order to actually release the boats was still not given.

Assessing his options, Captain Bartlett realised that his best chance lay in attempting to beach the vessel on the nearby island of Kea, but a failure of the steering gear meant that he could only turn the ship by using the engines. Even so, as *Britannic* once again started to move, the damaged forward compartments began to fill more rapidly; to further complicate matters, the ship began to take on an increasingly noticeable list to starboard. Barely fifteen minutes after the explosion the portholes on E deck, normally about 25ft above the waterline, were already beneath the surface, and the fact that many of them had been opened by the medical staff earlier that morning to ventilate the lower decks of the ship was now seriously compromising *Britannic*'s chances of survival. Ordering the engines stopped, Captain Bartlett decided that the priority was to get everybody safely off before making any further attempt to save the ship.

With the evacuation of *Britannic* continuing, help was already on the way. At 8.15 a.m. the destroyer HMS *Scourge*, while arranging for the beached Greek steamer *Sparti* to be towed after having struck a mine the previous day off the island of Phleva, had picked up *Britannic*'s SOS from Port St Nikolo. Ordering the French tugs *Goliath* and *Polyphemus* to follow, *Scourge*, under the command of Lieutenant Commander Henry Tupper, immediately set a course for the Kea Channel; twenty minutes later the destroyer HMS *Foxhound* was also signalled by *Scourge* to break off from her patrol in the Saronic Gulf in order to assist with the rescue.

But there was help even closer at hand. The auxiliary cruiser *Heroic*, under the command of Lieutenant

Major Harold Edgar Priestley had made his reputation long before joining *Britannic*. After being captured while serving with the 6th Field Ambulance during the retreat from Mons in August 1914, Priestley would eventually find himself in the Wittenberg prisoner-of-war camp in Saxony, where his actions would be instrumental in controlling an outbreak of typhus. Priestley was invalided home in February 1916 and, upon returning to active duty, his voyage on *Britannic* would be his first and, as it turned out, last. (Angus Mitchell Collection)

Forward section of *Britannic* where the explosion occurred. (Author)

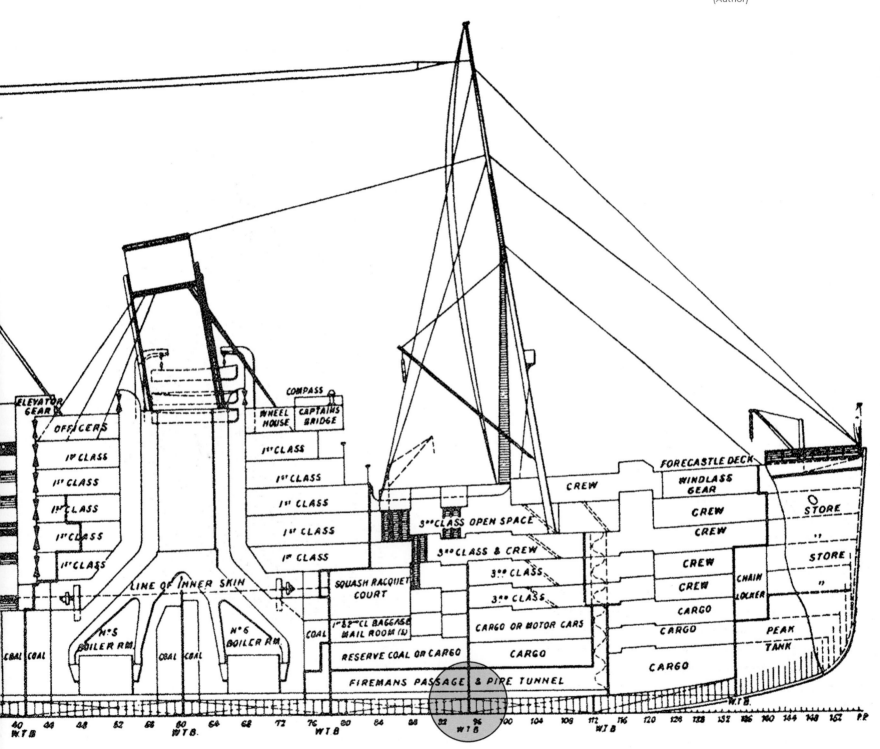

ELEVATOR GEAR

COMPASS

WHEEL HOUSE · CAPTAINS BRIDGE

OFFICERS

1ST CLASS

1ST CLASS

1ST CLASS

1ST CLASS

1ST CLASS

1ST CLASS

1ST CLASS

1ST CLASS

1ST CLASS

LINE OF INNER SKIN

SQUASH RACQUET COURT

1ST & 2ND CL BAGGAGE MAIL ROOM (S)

FORECASTLE DECK

CREW

WINDLASS GEAR

STORE

3RD CLASS OPEN SPACE

3RD CLASS & CREW

3RD CLASS

3RD CLASS

CREW

CREW

STORE

CREW

CREW

CHAIN LOCKER

COAL

Nº 5 BOILER RM

COAL   COAL   COAL

Nº 6 BOILER RM

COAL

CARGO OR MOTOR CARS

CARGO

CARGO

CARGO

PEAK TANK

RESERVE COAL OR CARGO

CARGO

FIREMANS PASSAGE & PIPE TUNNEL

W.T.B

COAL COAL

40   44   48   52   56   60   64   68   72   76   80   84   88   92   96   100   104   108   112   116   120   124   128   132   136   140   144   148   152   P.P.

W.T.B   W.T.B.   W.T.B   W.T.B   W.T.B

Commander Percival Ram, Royal Naval Reserve (RNR), had actually passed *Britannic* earlier that morning while en route from Mudros to Salamis. At 8.28 a.m., *Heroic* was just turning north towards Piraeus when *Britannic*'s distress signal was received and without hesitation Lieutenant Commander Ram immediately turned his ship around and headed straight back for the Kea Channel.

With help fast approaching, the evacuation on board continued in as orderly a manner as possible. Captain Harry Dyke, *Britannic*'s assistant commander, was arranging the lowering of the boats from the aft davits on the starboard boat deck and, as custom dictated, the nurses were placed at the head of the queue. As they were being counted into the boats by Ms Dowse, *Britannic*'s formidable matron and, as it happened, a veteran of both the Sudan and Boer Wars, one of the ship's medical officers later recalled their calm appearance:

> I know that women can be brave, but I never dreamed they could rise to such heights of cool, unflinching courage as those nurses did when under Miss Dowse, the matron, they lined up on deck like so many soldiers, and unconcernedly and calmly waited their turn to enter the boats. We men are proud of them, and we can only hope England will hear of their courage. They were magnificent.

Their patience as they awaited their turn on the promenade deck below, however, was not mirrored by a group of firemen, who had taken one of the boats from the poop deck without authority. Realising that their boat was not filled to anything like its full capacity, Captain Dyke rushed from his station, called down to them and ordered them to pick up a number of men who had already jumped overboard. He then returned to his station to continue evacuating the women; once all of the nurses were safe and accounted for, Ms Dowse finally stepped into her boat before it was lowered over the side.

The evacuation seemed to be going according to plan, but inevitably the day would be tinged with tragedy, although the variations in the exact details from the witnesses mean that we will probably never know exactly what went wrong. According to Fifth Officer Gordon Fielding, it was at about 8.30 a.m. that two of

Captain Harry William Dyke was the assistant commander on board *Britannic*, having served on *Olympic* since March 1913. Harry Dyke remains one of *Britannic*'s great enigmas, having resigned from the White Star Line in January 1917 for personal reasons. He died in January 1927. (Harold Roberts Collection)

52640 Private Henry Freebury was one of the unfortunate souls unable to escape from the suction as two of the ship's lifeboats were pulled into *Britannic*'s turning port propeller. His body was never recovered and his name is listed on the Commonwealth War Graves Commission memorial at Mikra, Thessaloniki. (Jennifer Clarke Collection)

the port lifeboats were lowered into the water without the authority of Third Officer Francis Laws, but because of the forward momentum of the ship they were unable to get clear. Violet Jessop's account is somewhat different. She recalled that by the time she reached the boat deck she was told that the nurses had already gone, and she could see those boats steadily drawing away from the ship, in spite of the fact that *Britannic* was still moving ahead.

The consequences, however, were tragically similar. Two lifeboats were unable to get clear from the ship's side and gradually drifted aft towards *Britannic*'s port propeller, which was by now turning above the surface. Seated in lifeboat no. 4, Violet later recalled:

A few minutes after the lifeboat first touched the water, every man jack in the group of surrounding boats took a flying leap into the sea. They came thudding from behind and all around me, taking to the water like a vast army of rats.

Not a word, not a shout was heard, just hundreds of men fleeing into the sea as if from an enemy in pursuit. It was extraordinary to find myself in the space of a few minutes the only occupant of the boat; I say almost, for one man, a doctor, was still standing in silence beside me. I turned around to see the reason for this exodus and, to my horror, saw *Britannic*'s huge propellers churning and mincing up everything near them – men, boats and everything were just one ghastly whirl.

Some were luckier than others. Young George Perman was able to grab hold of a hanging davit rope just in time and held on for dear life, but the scene he witnessed would leave emotional scars for years to come, as the propellers shattered human bodies and scattered pieces of debris in every direction. Within seconds both the surface of the water and the ship's white flanks were covered in streaks of blood.

Although Violet had never actually learned to swim, she quickly realised that it was now a case of either jumping into the sea and swimming for it, or suffering the same fate. In spite of her lifelong fear of drowning, she leapt overboard, the weight of her coat at first dragging her down into the depths for what seemed like an eternity. Then she began to feel herself rising, eventually coming up beneath one of the lifeboats, which prevented her from reaching the surface. Suddenly there was a terrific crash as something very solid struck her on the back of her head. She instinctively reached out for something to grab hold of, in an attempt to free herself from her predicament, when:

... joy of joys, I touched something – an arm – that moved as mine moved! My fingers gripped it like a vice, but only for a second, until my almost senseless head remembered what is said of the people drowning, that they retain their hold after death, bringing death to another. With that cheering thought, I let go.

After what seemed an eternity, but in reality was probably only a few seconds, Violet once again broke the surface. Grabbing hold of a loose lifejacket for support, she could finally open her eyes enough to be greeted by the sight of an unfortunate orderly, with his head split open and his brains trickling on to his khaki tunic. All around her she could see nothing but dead bodies, severed limbs and large pieces of debris, while the agonised cries of the wounded drowned out the sound of the now receding propellers.

Just as a third boat was about share a similar fate, as if by magic the propellers stopped. The sight of the now motionless 23ft propeller, which only seconds earlier had been wreaking bloody carnage, must have been a blessed one for Captain T. Fearnhead and the few remaining occupants of a third lifeboat which had almost shared the same fate. Fearnhead wasted no time in pushing hard against the stationary propeller blade to get clear in case they should suddenly start up again, while George Perman also seized the opportunity to escape from his predicament, sliding down the rope to which he had been desperately clinging before dropping into the water and swimming to a nearby lifeboat.

As the rescue work went on, *Britannic*'s officers continued to lower additional boats into the water, although the process was complicated by the fact that after the first boats had been successfully lowered, the forward set of port-side gantry davits had become inoperable. Concentrating on the aft set, Fifth Officer Fielding was still able to launch another three boats, one of which was commanded by First Officer H. Hollingsworth, a survivor of RMS *Arabic*, who had been ordered by Captain Bartlett to co-ordinate the rescue of the many swimmers in the water.

By about 8.45 a.m., the increasing list to starboard had made any further use of the port davits impossible, at which point the davit crews began to throw deck chairs and life rafts to the many swimmers below. Fielding was even contemplating the fact that in due course one of these rafts could well save his own life, when suddenly he saw Sixth Officer J. Chapman beside one of the smaller boats under the Welin davits; before long Fielding had helped to manhandle the boat into position and lower

Lieutenant John Cropper was a native of Chepstow. At the age of 50, Dr Cropper would have been too old for front-line service, but even so, at the outbreak of hostilities he enlisted in the RAMC, seeing service in the medical and transport departments at Boulogne, the Anglo Ethiopian Hospital at Frévent and at St Valery sur Somme. On 11 October 1916, Cropper extended his original contract with the RAMC for a further year, by which time he had been appointed to *Britannic*. (John Harvey Collection)

it into the water, finally escaping by dropping down the rope and into the lifeboat itself.

Even at this stage it seemed that *Britannic*, by some miracle, might still have been saved. Captain Bartlett noticed that the ship was not sinking as fast as before and, taking advantage of this unexpected respite, at 8.45 a.m. he ordered the engines to be restarted in a final attempt to reach land. Once again *Britannic* began to edge forward, but with the propellers by now working above the surface, the progress was inefficient and painfully slow. Even so, the forward motion was still enough to force the bow deeper and when reports began to arrive on the bridge that the water level had risen as high as D deck, Captain Bartlett knew that it could now only be

a matter of time. Resigning himself to the inevitable, he gave the signal for the engineers still working deep down in the engine room to come up on deck.

By this time the end was near, but even during these last desperate minutes men continued to go below. Percy Tyler made several trips below to fetch lifebelts for those who didn't have them, before helping to place one of the sea scouts 'rather forcibly' in a lifeboat, into which he was also ordered. It turned out to be the third-to-last boat to be lowered.

Rev. Fleming's escape was also something of a last-minute affair. He too had made a number of trips below to collect bread before helping the crew to throw the deck-chairs and life rafts over the side. He was finally ordered into the second-to-last lifeboat by Major Priestly, who, declining a seat himself, proceeded to take one last look around to make sure that everyone was safe. Priestly finally escaped a few minutes later in the last boat to be lowered, along with Claude Lancaster, *Britannic*'s purser, carrying the ship's log and papers with him.

As the waters steadily rose up over the bow and *Britannic* continued to heel over, Captain Bartlett sounded a final long blast on the ship's whistle, signalling the order to abandon ship, before simply walking off the starboard wing of the bridge and into the water. It was a timely signal for Chief Engineer Robert Fleming and the remaining engineers who, like their companions on *Titanic*, had remained at their stations until the last possible minute, escaping via the only possible escape route left to them: up the staircase and through the funnel casing of the fourth smoke stack, which actually served in part as a ventilator for the turbine engine room.

As the ship continued to heel over, one by one the funnels gave way under the strain as they crashed into the water. At 9.07 a.m., only fifty-five minutes after the explosion, *Britannic* finally rolled over to starboard as her stern slipped below the surface, leaving thirty-five boats and hundreds of survivors in the water, scattered over the now empty Kea Channel.

46907 Private Holmes Brelsford was in the last lifeboat to be lowered before *Britannic* sank. Formerly a Lancashire cotton weaver, he enlisted in the RAMC in November 1914 at the age of 20 and served with the British Expeditionary Force in France, before being invalided home suffering from bronchitis in June 1916. He joined *Britannic* on 24 September 1916. (Janet Baillie Collection)

7

RESCUE

Arthur Mee's Hero Book told the story of *Britannic*'s boy scouts, recording that even though they were young, they still insisted on being treated the same as the men. (TBF)

By 9.10 a.m. on the morning of Tuesday 21 November 1916, the previously calm and tranquil Kea Channel was covered with lifeboats and scores of swimmers, clinging to all manner of debris and life rafts that littered the surface. Fortunately, the combination of the warm water, calm conditions and a nearby island helped to ensure that the situation was far from hopeless, but even so, the favourable conditions left little room for complacency. Unlike Captain Smith, who had been receiving regular reports on the progress of *Titanic*'s rescuers, Captain Bartlett had little or no idea how far away any assistance might be. He might have been reasonably confident that his distress messages had got through, but due to a defect in the ship's receiving apparatus, possibly caused by the initial explosion, *Britannic*'s telegraphists had been unable to pick up any responses from the ships coming to their aid; to further complicate matters, the initial request for assistance 'off Port Nikolo' had also confused the issue due to the fact that there were a number of similarly named locations in the Aegean.

On the other hand, the Kea Channel was a relatively busy shipping area and before long the survivors would be reassured by the sight of columns of smoke of the fast-approaching aid, but in the meantime there were still dozens of wounded needing urgent attention. The carnage wrought by *Britannic*'s propeller was substantial and, although no one was known to have been killed in the initial explosion, it would later emerge that twenty-one of the ship's crew and nine officers and men of the RAMC had been killed in the two lifeboats pulled into the ship's side. With another forty men seriously wounded and little idea as to how long it would be before help arrived, Captain Bartlett ordered the two motor launches to collect as many wounded as possible and to make for the nearby island of Kea. Almost immediately Ms Dowse was organising her staff to make sure that the injured were properly cared for, even thinking to send half a dozen nurses ashore with the motor launches, where another 150 survivors, many of them badly wounded, were stranded.

Local help was already close at hand. Francesco Psilas, a fisherman from Port St Nikolo, was very quickly on the scene and he immediately began to give what little help he could, but by 10 a.m. HMS *Scourge* and HMS *Heroic* had arrived and had quickly lowered their boats in order

The 1,800grt *Heroic* was built in 1906 by Harland & Wolff and operated by the Belfast Steamship Company between Liverpool and Belfast. *Heroic* was requisitioned for military service but returned to Belfast at the end of the war. She was scrapped in 1952. (TBF)

HMS *Scourge* (top) and HMS *Foxhound* (below) were both Beagle (G) class destroyers; at 995 tons, *Foxhound* was slightly larger than *Scourge*, but both vessels were capable of 27 knots. The G class would become the last coal-burning destroyers in the Royal Navy and were scrapped in 1921. (TBF)

to begin their own rescue operations. Within two hours, *Heroic* had picked up nearly 500 survivors and space was fast running out on the *Scourge*, where another 339 survivors already filled most of the destroyer's 174ft deck. The situation was saved by the timely arrival of HMS *Foxhound* at 11.45 a.m., under the command of Lieutenant Commander William Shuttleworth; with the light cruiser HMS *Foresight* and the auxiliary cruiser HMS *Chasseur* also nearby, *Heroic* and *Scourge* secured their boats and headed north-west for Piraeus.

Ensuring that the channel was clear of survivors, Shuttleworth took his vessel into Port St Nikolo and, after dropping anchor at 1 p.m., immediately began to take the wounded on board. Within an hour HMS *Foresight* was also anchored in the harbour and, after sending medical officers to assist with the casualties, offered to take the wounded to Mudros. The attractions of the larger scout cruiser were all too obvious, but by that time all of the survivors, with the exception of Sergeant William Sharpe who had died of his injuries on the quayside, had been taken aboard *Foxhound*. The thought of transferring the wounded once again persuaded Shuttleworth that the original decision to take them to Piraeus was probably the best option and, weighing anchor at 2.15 p.m., *Foxhound* headed for the Greek mainland. Meanwhile, *Foresight* stayed behind to collect the remaining lifeboats and to arrange via the local French vice consul for the burial of Sergeant Sharpe.

Along with Sergeant Sharpe, three more men would fail to survive long enough to reach Piraeus. On board *Heroic* Private Arthur Binks of the RAMC and fireman Charles Phillips added to the day's list of casualties, while fireman

Joseph Brown would also succumb to his injuries aboard the French tug *Goliath*.

By mid-afternoon, the focus of all the activity had moved 40 miles to the north-west, when at 3.45 p.m. HMS *Heroic* arrived in the Bay of Salamis. After proceeding alongside the British flagship HMS *Duncan*, the second transfer of the survivors could begin. *Scourge* followed at 4 p.m. and, by the time *Foxhound* arrived alongside *Duncan* at 5.30 p.m., the battleship's sick bay was already filled to overflowing. As a result, after taking off the uninjured survivors, *Foxhound* cast off and proceeded to the military pier at Piraeus where the injured could be transferred to the nearby Russian hospital.

Faced with suddenly having to accommodate so many survivors, the logistics involved in clothing, housing and feeding over 1,000 unexpected personnel were formidable, but by the end of the evening some semblance of order had been restored. With the help of Admiral Gabriel Darrieus, commander of the French 3rd Squadron, a number of the survivors were dispersed around the French ships, while others found themselves quartered on the ex-Austrian Lloyd steamer *Marienbad* and the ex-Greek torpedo depot ship *Kanaris*; some of the more fortunate ship's officers found themselves quartered aboard HMS *Duncan* in order to assist with the inquiry, while others found themselves transferred to hotels at nearby Phaleron. Meanwhile, *Britannic*'s nurses, after tea aboard the flagship with Rear Admiral Arthur Hayes-Sadler, would find themselves quartered in the Aktaion Hotel, where, courtesy of a car organised by the British port control officer at Piraeus, they could assist in helping the wounded at the Russian hospital.

From this point onwards, *Britannic*'s crew and medical staff would be separated as the various branches of the military pondered on how best to repatriate them. For one brief moment on the afternoon of 22 November they were reunited at the local graveyard to attend the burials of Private Binks and Firemen Phillips and Brown, although sadly by now the name of George Honeycott, one of *Britannic*'s lookouts, had also been added to the list of the killed, having died from his wounds the previous evening at the Russian hospital.

There still remained the task of completing the inquiry into *Britannic*'s loss. Captain Bartlett and the senior

Although closed for the winter, the Aktaion Hotel was still able to accommodate *Britannic*'s eighty nurses, even though they had originally expected only eighteen. (Angus Mitchell Collection)

AKTAION PALACE HOTEL

ΦΑΛΗΡΟΝ · ΑΘΗΝΑΙ
PHALÈRE · ATHÈNES

DIRECTEUR: S. STYLIANOS.

officers had remained aboard HMS *Duncan* in order to assist Captain Hugh Heard and his chief engineering officer, Commander George Staer, with their inquiries, but by 24 November the task was as complete as it reasonably could be. Their report to Rear Admiral Hayes-Sadler did not attempt to cover up its own shortcomings, which had been made all the more complicated by the fact that few of the witnesses had seen anything in the lead-up to the explosion, and the near-impossibility of locating so many survivors scattered around the fleet and Athens in the short period of time available.

The report itself was reasonably conclusive in that there had been a single explosion, but the conflicting evidence from several of the witnesses meant that the actual cause was by no means certain. Deck Steward Thomas Walters, who had once served as an officer's steward in the Royal Navy, remained convinced that he had seen the track of an approaching torpedo on the starboard side. Indeed, the case for the torpedo seemed to gain further credence from the testimony of Assistant Baker Henry Etches, who had been on another part of the deck at the time; crucially, though, he saw his torpedo much further aft and on the port side of the ship. Torpedo sightings were not uncommon in these circumstances and there is probably little doubt that Walters and Etches were genuinely convinced that they had seen one, but as their statements failed to agree as to which side it had been observed, their evidence could hardly claim to be conclusive. Heard also noted that there was no report from anyone on the bridge of a column of water being thrown up following the explosion, which was customary with torpedoes. If anything, this strongly suggested that the explosion had occurred directly beneath the ship, indicating that it was almost certainly caused by a mine. In the end, the final line of the inquiry more or less exonerated the Germans from the deliberate sinking of *Britannic*, concluding: 'The effects of the explosion might have been due to either a mine or a torpedo. The probability seems to be a mine.'

The British press, however, were not prepared to wait for so long before pronouncing their own verdict. On 23 November the first public accounts of what had happened began to surface and, with the available information vague at best, *The Times* simply reported

the preliminary Admiralty statement, which listed 1,106 survivors while estimating about fifty actually killed. The *Daily Mirror* made little effort to ascertain the actual facts and reported that every effort had been made to save over 1,000 sick and wounded, oblivious to the fact that the ship had actually been outward bound and had therefore been carrying no wounded at the time of her loss. Inevitably, there was little or nothing that the Germans could do to justify any attack on a hospital ship protected by the Hague Convention, except to muddy the already opaque waters with an official communiqué from Berlin in *The Times* claiming:

> According to reports so far at hand, the ship was on its way from England to Salonika. For a journey in this direction the large number of persons on board is extraordinarily striking, which justifies the forcible suspicion of the misuse of the hospital ship for purposes of transport. Inasmuch as the ship carried distinguishing marks of a hospital ship, in accordance with regulations, there can naturally be no question of a German submarine in connection with the sinking.

To counter the German allegation, the Admiralty published in the same edition of *The Times* their

A group of survivors visiting the Parthenon in Athens. Both of *Britannic*'s chaplains, James Atkinson and John Fleming, were able to enjoy the excursion. (Angus Mitchell Collection)

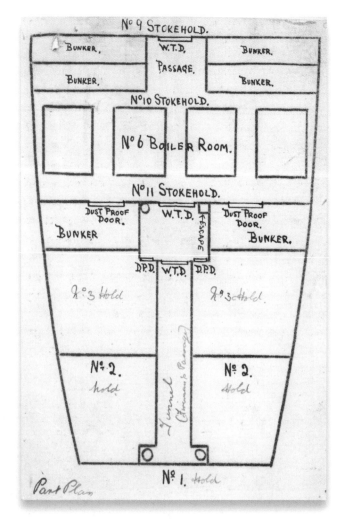

Several sketches from the inquiry held aboard HMS *Duncan*. These diagrams were the only technical resources to which Captain Heard and Commander Staer could refer before reaching their conclusions. (National Archives)

justification for so many personnel being on board. Of the 1,125 listed as being on board at the time, 625 were members of the ship's crew while the remaining 500 were described as medical staff, consisting of twenty-five officers (RAMC), seventy-six nurses and 399 medical orderlies, lab attendants and clerical staff. One can only wonder what the Germans would have made of the figures if *Britannic* had been sunk on her previous voyage, when she had in fact been transporting nearly 500 other medical staff to foreign stations.

But none of this would have mattered to the ship's crew and medical staff, by now marooned in Greece. With the political situation in Athens already on the point of exploding, the British authorities were keen to evacuate the civilians as soon as possible and, after only three days in Athens, on 24 November *Britannic*'s surviving officers and crew were transferred aboard RFA *Ermine*. The journey took the better part of two days, but after arriving at Mudros the survivors were given their first proper meal in days and the chance for a quick bath before going aboard the transport *Royal George*, which departed for Marseilles the following day.

Royal George reached Marseilles after a five-day voyage and it was here that Captain Bartlett finally bade farewell to his crew, before taking a scheduled passenger train to the northern French coast. For the remainder of the crew,

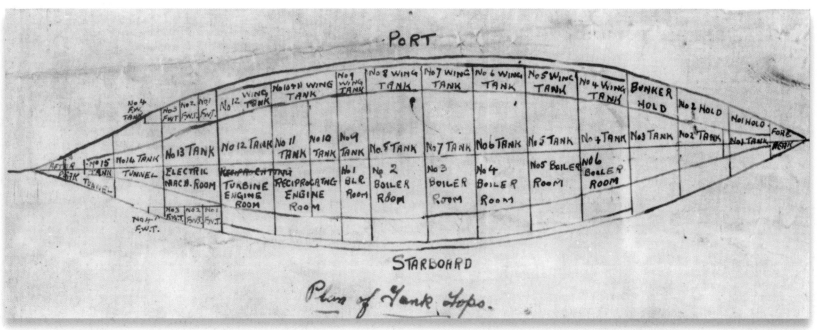

however, it was the beginning of a four-day ordeal. Leaving Marseilles a little after 5.30 p.m. on 4 December and crammed into unheated carriages, brief stops at Louvre, Lyon, Macon, Dijon and Nantes offered little in the way of warmth or refreshment other than the occasional mug of black tea. At Louvre the discipline seemed to break down altogether and the crew reportedly rushed the carriage containing the rations of bully beef and biscuits; the officers, or at least those who had any money with them, were able to find a passable meal at a local hotel, while a one-hour stop at Nantes also provided the opportunity for a welcome wash and brush-up.

The fifty-hour ordeal finally ended when the train pulled into the station at Le Havre shortly after 8 p.m. on 6 December. After that it was a 5-mile march to the camp and another freezing night, this time on bare wooden boards under canvas without even a blanket. It was so cold that for many of the men sleep was impossible and they only got through the night by running around the camp in an attempt to keep warm. The following morning the men were given a meagre breakfast, but later that afternoon, following a meal of hot stew and bread, the men completed a final 6-mile march to Le Havre before finally embarking on the transport *Caesarea*. After an uneventful crossing they arrived back at Southampton at 9 a.m. on 8 December, where the privations of the last two weeks were probably offset when Captain Bartlett greeted them with the news that due to their conduct on the day of the sinking any fines that had been previously imposed on errant crew members had been cancelled. On top of that, everyone would also be granted the usual two weeks' survivors' leave.

For the medical staff the nightmare journey home wasn't much different. Along with the wounded, they were transferred aboard the hospital ship *Grantully Castle* at Piraeus on 27 November for transportation to Malta, before eventual repatriation to England via troop transports to Marseilles.

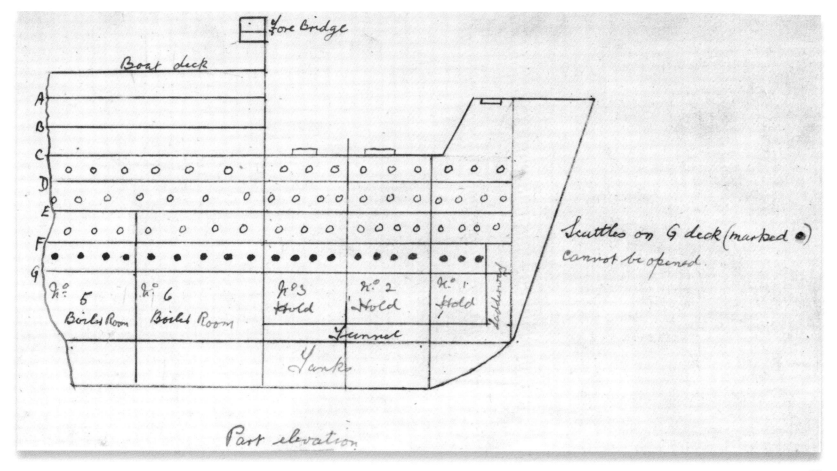

Percy Tyler's journal of his journey home reads much the same as the description of the crew's ordeal. After ten days on Malta, on the morning of 10 December the men of the RAMC went aboard the transport *Huntsend*, bound for Marseilles, but due to stormy weather and the zigzag course the ship did not arrive at her destination until the evening of 16 December. Once at Marseilles the same nightmare train journey to Le Havre was repeated, with nine men packed into compartments of barely 40sq. ft, and from then on it was the same story of freezing weather, meagre rations, black tea and cigarettes. The train reached Le Havre during the early hours of 20 December, but it was not until the evening that the men finally boarded the transport *King Edward*, bound for Southampton, where they finally arrived at 10.30 a.m. the following morning, exactly one month after *Britannic* had met her fate.

The nurses had it somewhat easier. To be spared the hardships of the overland route, they were held back on Malta until the hospital ship *Valdivia* was available to transport them in relative safety to England. Even so, the voyage home would be a far cry to the relative comfort that the nurses had enjoyed aboard *Britannic*, as Sheila Macbeth's diary would recall:

After being seventeen days on the island, we were hurried on board H.M.H.S. *Valdivia*, which is usually a French cargo-boat. In peacetime it is probably a nice boat to sail on, but without cargo and with empty water tanks, it was a beast and rolled about, as much as it could, without rolling completely over. We slept (or at least tried to do so with very little success) in different Wards. I was with my friends in a Ward with about a hundred Sisters. The Ward contained three baths, all out of use for lack of water and three small wash-basins. We started to get up at 5 a.m. so that each one might get a 'sponge.' As I went to the second breakfast, I seldom got a look at the washing-place until late, when the Orderlies were running about – so I had to wash with one hand and cling to the screen with the other for fear of being left high and dry after each roll!!!

Between the rough sea and the rolling, we shipped two seas in our Ward and so were forced to keep the portholes shut. You may imagine how hot and stuffy it became, and why I would not be persuaded to stay in bed and 'go sick' when I hit my head on the hatchway, but rather preferred to lie on the deck pillowed by my waistcoat. There were only about a dozen chairs between 150 or more people, so many of us went about in terror of arriving in England with 'deck sores!'

The boat had come from Egypt and had hoped to get water at Malta. Getting none there, we called for it at Gibraltar, where we got none either – so we had to drink several lots of tea and coffee made with salt water before we arrived at Southampton

THE WAR.

LOSS OF A BRITISH HOSPITAL SHIP.

THE "BRITANNIC" SUNK IN THE ÆGEAN SEA.

The Secretary of the Admiralty made the following announcement yesterday afternoon :—

The British hospital ship *Britannic* was sunk by mine or torpedo yesterday morning (Tuesday, Nov. 21) in the Zea Channel, in the Ægean Sea.

There are 1106 survivors, 28 of whom are injured, and it is estimated that about 50 are lost.

Full particulars will be published as soon as they are received.

ATHENS, Nov. 21.

According to the latest information received the *Britannic* lowered all her boats, numbering 35, and every effort was made to save the sick and wounded, who are said to have numbered upwards of a thousand.

The vessel was apparently coming from Salonica. It is reported that but few lives were lost.

Full particulars are not yet available.—*Reuter*.

[The *Britannic* was one of the largest liners flying the British Mercantile flag and was constructed for the White Star Line by Messrs. Harland & Wolff, Ltd. of Belfast, to replace the ill-starred *Titanic*. She was completed in 1915, and her dimensions were 852.5 ft. by 94 ft. by 59.6 ft., and her tonnage was 48,185 gross and 24,592 net. She was launched in 1914 and cost over £1,500,000.]

Lloyds List of Thursday 23 November 1916 could only report the basic information that had been received. (Author)

on Boxing Day. The whole of the voyage we had to hug the coastline for fear of submarines, and so ran out of many things such as biscuits, ginger beer and oranges – in fact, they were the only things I really wanted considering the way I felt.

On Christmas Day we were quite a gay crowd and quite determined to throttle all talk of home and make the best of a bad job. Many had hung their stockings up and found a varied assortment of presents in them, such as soap, half a comb, cigarettes, a patent leather belt, chocolate, oranges, and nailbrushes, etc., in fact whatever we had or could get at the canteen. Our dear old Matron had a present for each of us, which she had brought from Malta. I got a pretty blue and white Kimono and, in consequence and also because we played a lot of wild games, took twice as long to get to bed that night. The thought of getting home on the morrow made everyone hilarious and so the 'stodgy' girls were teased and put in the ice chests to punish them for not being excited.

On Boxing Day we got into Southampton about 9 a.m. and left the boat after lunch as she had to go off to France that afternoon instead of going out

Taken at Salonika on 26 November 1916, a group of *Britannic* survivors were photographed on the foredeck of the battleship HMS *Lord Nelson*. (TBF)

The nurses and some of
Britannic's medical officers
are photographed outside the
Aktaion Hotel in Piraeus. (Angus
Mitchell Collection)

into dry dock for repairs. We all crowded into the Waterloo train, where we were met by Miss Becher (The Matron-in-Chief) who told us that we might proceed to our homes to await further orders.

So ended my days as a refugee, at any rate for this trip.

By the end of the Christmas holiday all of the survivors were safely home, but while in time they would find themselves posted to other ships or theatres of war, as far as *Britannic* was concerned the end of 1916 was by no means the end of the story.

Right: Having transferred hundreds of invalids into *Britannic* on numerous occasions, on 27 November the medical staff and nurses boarded HMHS *Grantully Castle* for the two-day journey to Malta. (Angus Mitchell Collection)

Below: On 30 November 1916, *Britannic*'s surviving medical staff assembled one last time for this group shot, taken at Fort Manoel on Malta. (Angus Mitchell Collection)

Below: To be spared the rigours of the overland journey, the nurses were held at Malta until HMHS *Valdivia* was ready to return to England, arriving back at Southampton on Boxing Day 1916. (Angus Mitchell Collection)

Right: After the war the Admiralty endeavoured to recover as much of its expenditure as possible, which included auctioning off the unused wooden panelling that had not been installed in *Britannic* before the ship was requisitioned. (David Hutchings Collection)

H.M. HOSPITAL SHIP "VALDIVIA"   (Publication Officially sanctioned by the Lords Commissioners of the Admiralty.)

OFFICIAL NOTICES

G.   R.

BELFAST.

By direction of the Lords Commissioners of the Admiralty.

Second and most Important Sale by Auction

of the valuable Unused

SS. "BRITANNIC" EQUIPMENT,

on Tuesday, 26th August, 1919, and following day, if necessary.

Including, as previously advertised, the costly Carved Austrian Oak, Mahogany, Sycamore and Walnut Panelling in "Louis," "Georgian," "Jacobean" and "Adam" Styles.

Pilasters, Mouldings, Cornicing, Counters, Fireplaces, &c., Lincrusta, Fibrous Plaster, and three-ply Ceiling Panellings, &c.

Several Hundred Ships' Fitment Wardrobes, Toilet Tables, Door Frames, Doors, Bookcases, Sideboards, &c.

Large Quantities Pine and other Quartering, Framing Sheeting and Arisings, as removed from Storage.

Descriptive Catalogues, giving full particulars, price 2/- each, from

W. P. GRAY & MacDOWELL, LTD.,
Government Auctioneers and Valuers,
Chichester Street, Belfast.

Phone 99.   Wires—"Realise," Belfast.

8

AFTERMATH

Following the loss of the
Britannic, Charles Bartlett
returned to his shore-based
duties with the White Star Line.
In 1921 he was invested with the
CBE and he retired from the
company on 31 December 1931. H
died in Liverpool on 15 February
1945, aged 76. (Alasdair Fairbairn
Collection)

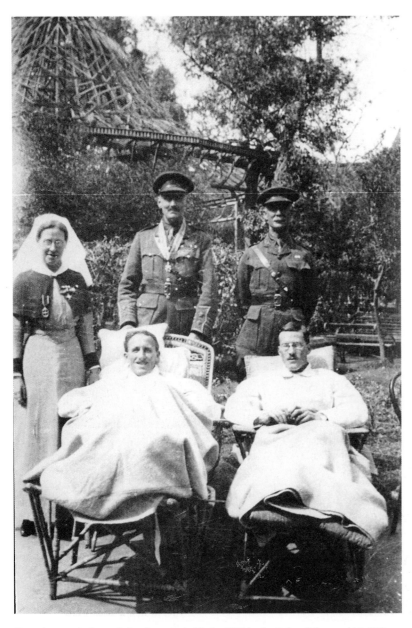

Henry Stewart Anderson being decorated with the CMG by the Duke of Connaught in 1918. Anderson returned quickly to active duty following *Britannic*'s loss and in January 1917 he was made the senior medical officer at the Citadel Hospital in Cairo, where he would remain until the end of 1921. After returning to England he was placed on retired pay in 1924 but continued to serve as medical officer at the army's Northampton depot until 1937. Henry Anderson died on 24 May 1961, aged 89, but unusually he chose to leave his body for medical research. (Llewellyn Lloyd Collection)

Following *Britannic*'s loss, Harold Priestly saw further service in hospital ships, followed by postings to Bristol and Lyndhurst. After the war he went on to serve in Singapore and Lahore before retiring early due to ill health in 1932. Priestley never fully recovered from the pleurisy which he contracted at Wittenberg, and he died from pulmonary and renal tuberculosis at his home in Yately, Hampshire, on 16 March 1941, aged 62. (Army Medical Services Museum)

Following the loss of *Britannic*, Holmes Brelsford was posted to Salonika in January 1917, where he would remain for the rest of the war. After returning to England he would work in the Burnley coal mines and later as a bath engineer in Morecambe. The above uniform is that of the St John's Ambulance Brigade, and he also wears his war decorations, including the 14–15 Star, War and Victory medals – the trio of medals nicknamed 'Pip, Squeak and Wilfred' after the cartoon strip in the *Daily Mirror*. Holmes Brelsford died on 27 April 1963, aged 69. (Janet Baillie Collection)

After returning to Britain, John Fleming saw further service in Belgium, France and Palestine. After the war he served as minister in Dundee, Doune and Abernethy. He died at Stracathro on 4 May 1953, aged 71. (John Fleming Collection)

Unlike *Titanic*, you will not find any memorials dedicated to *Britannic*. There has never been any detailed public scrutiny of the ship's loss, no mass gravesite for the victims and little to remind the public that the ship ever existed.

Britannic can never be linked with an event of anything like the magnitude with which we all associate *Titanic* or *Lusitania*, and although at 48,157grt *Britannic* is by far the largest British mercantile vessel to be sunk in either of the two world wars – bearing in mind the 5,000 Allied vessels amounting to over 11 million tons that were sent to the bottom between 1914 and 1918 – there can be little surprise that *Britannic* was seen as barely more than a statistic. In every conceivable way, *Britannic* was just one of many vessels in the wrong place at the wrong time.

There was a brief bureaucratic afterlife as the White Star Line tied up the few remaining loose ends with the British Government, but the issue of insurance was relatively straightforward. *Britannic* had been lost as a direct result of a war risk and while on government service, which meant that White Star would be compensated in full for their losses; all that remained to be done was calculate the final sum. The Admiralty actually made the initial down payment of £1.75 million as early as 23 January 1917, but it was not until March 1917 that Harland & Wolff finally completed their calculations and White Star were able to present a precise breakdown of the figure, which amounted to £1,947,797 5s. By the end of May 1917 the final payments for *Britannic*, *Laurentic* and *Afric*, all lost while in government service and amounting to £600,000, had still not fully been met, and so the following month a

After the war Violet Jessop (rear row, far right) would see further service with the White Star and Royal Mail Lines, before retiring from the sea in 1950 and moving to Suffolk. She died in May 1971, aged 83. (Margaret & Mary Meehan Collection)

further £100,000 was advanced to the company until the Admiralty had completed its own calculations.

By the summer of 1917, *Britannic* was little more than history: the White Star Line had been compensated, the five recovered casualties were buried in their corner of a foreign field, and the survivors had been repatriated and reassigned. For Captain Bartlett this meant a return to his shore duties as White Star Marine Superintendent at Liverpool, and for Lieutenant Colonel Anderson it was a posting to Cairo, where in January 1917 he would assume command of the Citadel Military Hospital until the end of the war. Major Harold Priestley would initially return to the

world of hospital ships, being reassigned to HMHS *Egypt*, while Matron Elizabeth Dowse, after extended sick leave, would depart for her next posting in May 1917 at 39 Stationary Hospital, located at Aire, in the Pas de Calais. This posting would last just over a month before she was once again transferred, this time to 79 General Hospital at Taranto, Italy, where she would remain for the rest of the war.

Britannic's crew would also find new ships, many, according to legend, taking berths in HMT *Justicia*, but the devastation wrought by *Britannic*'s port propeller meant that at least eight of the injured survivors would never

After returning to England, George Perman became an electrical apprentice at the Thornycroft shipyard at Woolston, Hampshire, before joining the Royal Mail Line as an electrician. After seven years at sea George entered the church, later becoming minister at the Smithfield Martyrs memorial church in London, and then vicar at St Mary's church, Ealing. The last known living link with *Britannic*, George Heyward Perman died at the Koinonia Christian Rest Home in Worthing on 24 May 2000, aged 99. (Author)

Sheila Macbeth would later find herself posted to hospitals in France, where she would remain until 1918. She would marry in 1920 and move to India, before later becoming one of Scotland's best-known genealogists, for which she would be awarded the MBE in 1980. Intriguingly, Sheila returned to *Britannic* in 1976 as the guest of Jacques Cousteau and even descended to the wreck in the *Calypso*'s submersible, *Soucoupe*. She died at Batheaston on 15 February 1994, aged 103. (Angus Mitchell Collection)

Casualty Form—Active Service. Army Form B. 103. Regiment or Corps: RAMC (N.A.) Regimental No. 81292 Rank Pt. Name Bostock, Geo. James. Enlisted 1.11.15 Terms of Service D.o.W. Service reckons from 1-11-15. Record: Missing after ship sank — Britannic — Zea Channel — 21/11/16.

One of the scattered service records relating to 81292 Private George James Bostock. With so many British Army service records destroyed during the Blitz, little information on the nine officers and men of the RAMC can be easily found today. (Author)

serve at sea again. As a small recompense for their loss, the Board of Trade had the right to award a decoration known as the Silver War Badge to any master, officer or seaman in the British merchant marine, provided that they were considered to be permanently incapacitated for service due to enemy action. In the end, these eight were included in the register of merchant seamen granted the Silver War Badge; the nature of their individual injury was also recorded:

> (Case 9) J. Herring (2nd Cook): Amputation of left leg above knee; injury caused by being struck by the propeller after vessel had been mined or torpedoed.
>
> (Case 22) W. Kneller (Fireman): Compound fracture of left leg caused by being struck by propeller while in the water after vessel had been mined or torpedoed.
>
> (Case 23) G. Sherratt (Assistant Laundryman): Amputation of left leg as result of injury received by being struck by propeller while in the water after vessel had been mined or torpedoed.

> (Case 24) C.G. Sparks (Fireman): Amputation of right leg; struck by propeller while in the water after vessel had been mined or torpedoed.
>
> (Case 47) R.E. Bennett (Leading Fireman): Struck by propeller while in the water after the vessel was torpedoed or mined; back of both legs injured.
>
> (Case 48) E.G.C. Long (Engineer's Storekeeper): Struck by propeller when in the water after the vessel was torpedoed; injury to abdomen and lower ribs of right side.
>
> (Case 49) T.W. Mitchell (Fireman): Struck by propeller while in the water after the vessel was torpedoed or mined; compound fracture of left leg.
>
> (Case 67) P. Healey (Trimmer): Right leg injured by propeller while in the water after the vessel had been mined or torpedoed.

Even so, the seriousness of a crewman's individual injury was not always as straightforward as might have been imagined, and laundryman G. Sherratt might have felt particularly aggrieved when at one stage the Board of Trade considered it questionable as to whether or not he could be considered as being 'incapacitated' by his injury – the loss of his left leg – from performing the duties of laundryman on board a ship. In the end, the Board, in its infinite generosity, gave Sherratt 'the benefit of the doubt'.

And so Britannic faded into history and became all but forgotten. The name, however, was not, and in 1930 MV Britannic entered service as the third and, as it would turn out, final White Star liner to bear the name. The third Britannic would remain on the North Atlantic mail run until the end of 1960, when, as the final serving White Star liner, she was scrapped at Inverkeithing.

Meanwhile, her illustrious predecessor rested quietly, 400ft beneath the surface of the Kea Channel, waiting to be rediscovered.

The War of 1914–1918.

Royal Army Medical Corps

T/Capt. (A/Maj.) H. Goodman, 76th Fd. Amb.

was mentioned in a Despatch from

Field Marshal Sir Douglas Haig, K.T. G.C.B. O.M. G.C.V.O. K.C.I.E.

dated 16th March 1919

for gallant and distinguished services in the Field.

I have it in command from the King to record His Majesty's

high appreciation of the services rendered.

Winston Churchill

War Office
Whitehall, S.W.
1st July 1919.

Secretary of State for War.

Although not aboard *Britannic* on the day of the sinking, Dr Harold Goodman would go on to serve in France with 76 Field Ambulance and was Mentioned in Dispatches by Field Marshal Haig on 16 March 1919. The certificate was signed by Winston Churchill, then Secretary of State for War. Harold Goodman died in Devon on 13 February 1957. (Ronald Goodman Collection)

The Cross of Sacrifice at Mikra, Thessaloniki, where the names of the eight missing RAMC officers and men aboard HMHS *Britannic* were commemorated. (Author)

H. S. BRITANNIC
ROYAL ARMY MEDICAL CORPS

CAPTAIN	PRIVATE
CROPPER J.	BOSTOCK G J.
	FREEBURY H.
SERJEANT	JONES T.
SHARPE W.	KING G.W.
	SMITH L.
	STONE W.

The grave of *Britannic*'s matron,
Elizabeth Ann Dowse, buried
in Fleet Cemetery in June 1941.
(Author)

The Merchant Marine Memorial at Tower Hill, London, lists the eighteen members of *Britannic*'s crew killed in the lifeboats and whose bodies were never recovered. (Author)

The original resting place of Sergeant William Sharpe in the St Trias churchyard, Port St Nikolo on Kea. Sergeant Sharpe's body was moved to the New British Cemetery on Syra in 1921, but due to a bureaucratic glitch, his name was incorrectly recorded and for eighty-nine years the grave carried the simple marker 'Known unto God'. On 31 December 2008 the British Ministry of Defence acknowledged the oversight and a new headstone was placed on the grave in 2009. (Author)

THE TWENTY-FIRST
CENTURY

H.M. Hospital Ship "BRITANNIC."

This contemporary, hand-tinted photograph sold on board comes as close as reasonably possible to verifying *Britannic*'s final colour scheme as a hospital ship, with the green band and yellow funnels. The date and location are unclear, but considering the overall condition of the paintwork and the extent of the work on the ship's shade deck, it is safe to assume that it was taken during her first period of service. (John Fleming Collection)

For almost sixty years the wreck of *Britannic* lay forgotten and undisturbed, but just occasionally there were brief reminders of her existence. These momentary glimpses, however, were fleeting at best and as a result two post-war surveys of the area by the Royal Navy effectively succeeded in the wreck being misplaced altogether. It was not until December 1975 that Captain Jacques Cousteau finally pinpointed the site, some 8 miles from her charted position and, interestingly, surprisingly close to the position recorded in the ship's 1916 log book.

Cousteau led a follow-up expedition with manned divers to the wreck in 1976, even though the underwater technology of the time allowed for little more than a brief glimpse, but it would be a further twenty years before Dr Robert Ballard would survey the wreck site in closer detail using ROV technology. Since then a further six expeditions carried out by manned divers and scientists have helped to show *Britannic* in an altogether different light.

In spite of the fact that there have been eight major explorations of the wreck between 1975 and 2008, little is known of the scientific data that has been accumulated. While the wreck of the more glamorous *Titanic* has continued to capture the imagination of the public and the scientists, work has continued quietly on *Britannic*

The preserved slipways at Belfast, where *Olympic*, *Titanic* and *Britannic* were all built. (Author)

and the resulting comparison of the two wreck sites has revealed two remarkably different environments, yet each is a fascinating ecosystem in its own right. *Titanic* lies 2½ miles down at the bottom of the Atlantic, her broken hull in a dark, cold and seemingly lifeless environment, and yet when the wreck was surveyed in 1986 Dr Robert Ballard identified what he termed 'rusticles'. At first sight these rusticles – so called because they look like icicles of rust – look like rusting iron, but in fact they are composed of iron-eating microbes that are literally feeding off the iron in *Titanic*'s hull plates, to the point where the deterioration of the iron plates will one day cause the wreck to collapse.

Britannic, on the other hand, appears to be a complete paradox when compared to her sister. Instead of a twisted, broken wreck, at first we are greeted by the sight of a ship lying in relatively shallow water, where you would naturally assume that the combination of natural light and organic sea life would by now have reduced the structure to a pile of indistinguishable plates. Yet none of this appears to be the case. Instead, *Britannic* is almost completely intact, with some observers commenting that if the sea life could be cleared from the wreck then she could even be raised and put on display. Perhaps this particular dream is a little far-fetched, but even so a study of the *Britannic* wreck is fascinating in its own right.

In 2008 the first real attempt to analyse the fauna and flora on and around *Britannic* was undertaken by the Hellenic Centre for Marine Research (Elkethe), the long-term goal of the analysis being to determine the potential for shipwrecks or manmade structures to function as artificial reefs. The logical starting point was to study the effect that the marine environment has had on *Britannic*'s hull, as surfaces exposed to a marine environment typically develop a layer of attached organisms as inorganic material settles, followed by the settlement of algae and bacteria. This process is known as 'biofouling' and over a period of time a complex and diverse community of fauna and flora will develop.

Britannic is located at the southernmost point of Attica in the Kea Channel, lying on a gentle slope that varies between 105m and 114m in depth. Around the shipwreck the predominant sediments are flat, muddy sand with discontinuous maerl (red coralline algae), sand and gravel. Generally the Kea Channel is a featureless, uninhabited desert and yet *Britannic* has been transformed into an artificial reef, creating an oasis of life and supporting a complex marine habitat and ecosystem. The shallowest part of the wreck lies at a depth of approximately 85m, the maximum depth of the seabed being measured at approximately 114m, but although the wreck is completely covered by settled fauna and flora, there are noticeable differences from top to bottom.

All of the main seabed organisms that now live on *Britannic* are filter feeders, including sponges, bivalves (clams), bryozoans (aquatic invertebrates) and tunicates (filter feeders). At the topmost part of the wreck there are colonies of marine worms and sponges, while the upper edge of the wreck is dominated by a variety of sponges. Below this area to the seabed lies a flatter level of biofouling, made up of smaller sponges, hard and soft red coralline algae, with some apparent green algae and saddle oysters. Adjacent to the hull is a low shelf comprised predominately of saddle oysters and maerl, probably resulting from fall-off from the wreck, while the fish inhabiting the wreck comprise numerous different species, predominantly Anthias; the occasional lobster can also be seen lurking in portholes on the upper port side of the vessel. On the other hand, the underside of the wreck, where the light level is lower, is dominated by saddle oysters and other small fouling organisms.

In that the hull was predominantly constructed from the same type of steel, the differences in the fouling communities seen on the wreck are probably due to environmental factors such as light, depth, surface orientation and the habitat's exposure to currents. However, the presence of mainly filter feeders, as found on *Britannic*, suggests that the composition of the benthic communities on an artificial substrate is different to those on natural hard-bottomed communities.

So what does all this science mean for *Britannic*?

Scientific research on RMS *Titanic* has been on-going since 1991, when biological activity reaction testers (BARTs), designed to detect and evaluate iron bacteria, were first employed on the wreck to determine that microbial activity existed within the rusticles, and to determine the rate of bio-deterioration. In September 2003 a similar battery of tests was instigated on *Britannic*, where, since November 1916, a growing mass of iron-rich

bio-concretions had accumulated on both the interior and exterior steel surfaces of the wreck.

Microscopic examination of the rusticles revealed that the structure was an extremely tight matrix of almost mat-like growth. Due to the less extreme environment found at the site, *Britannic*'s rusticles appeared quite different to those previously seen on *Titanic*, being similar to the complex structure of channels, reservoirs and crystalline structures, but within a more compact and tightly woven

After years in a private house, the philharmonic organ, originally manufactured by M. Welte & Söhne of Freiburg/Breisgau, was restored in 2007 and can now be seen at the Museum für Musikautomaten, at Seewen in Switzerland. (David Rumsey)

Korissia, Port St Nikolo, at night. (Antonello Paone)

matrix. This variation of growth has been put down to the conditions found on site, with the increased nutrient loading and the low levels of ambient light penetration at the depth of 400ft allowing a much wider group of organisms to be able to compete for nutrients, gases and habitat. Because of this, *Britannic*'s rusticles are not the dominant organisms on the wreck and they have adapted to their surroundings, becoming more defensive in nature.

The BART test platform was also used to determine the types and aggressiveness of the different groups of bacteria found on the wreck. In the seventy-two-hour period when the testers were exposed to the ambient nutrient flow, gases, currents and light, analysis of the results showed that the SRB (sulphate-reducing bacteria), IRB (iron-related bacteria) and SLYM (slime-forming bacteria) tests all indicated a highly aggressive environment. Slide film incorporated into the test platform also indicated that the bacterial elements were extremely aggressive, removing over 90 per cent of the gelatine emulsion in a three-day period.

By the end of 2003 researchers were beginning to see the wood for the trees. In spite of appearances, *Britannic* was showing evidence of significant deterioration due to the activities of the rusticles at the site. The rate at which the iron in the steels of the ship's structure were corroding would require further investigation and a steel platform was positioned on the wreck, near the forward port-side first-class entrance, where it would remain undisturbed for at least five years. In May 2009 the platform was retrieved, and the initial findings after sixty-nine months were clear: there was a more intense growth on the underside of the steel; rusticles were growing down from the individual steel coupons; and the resulting biomass was very irregular in form, unlike that on the recovered RMS *Titanic* platforms.

The coupons also demonstrated three types of corrosion, including perforation of the steel, lateral dishing of the steel surface and lateral line perforations along the narrowed side of the coupons. All of these events could be explained as microbiologically influenced corrosion,

In 1976 Captain Jacques Cousteau visited the Kea Channel to carry out the first examination of the wreck since *Britannic*'s loss sixty years earlier. It was Cousteau who confirmed that *Britannic*'s holds were empty, disproving the legend that the hospital ship had been carrying munitions and supplies for the troops. Here the support team are preparing *Calypso*'s submersible, *Soucoupe*, which was rated to a depth of 350m. (Titanic Historical Society)

with the evidence clearly indicating that the environment on *Britannic* was conducive to microbe-induced corrosion. Perhaps that should be no surprise, as nearly all metal objects placed in a warm and relatively shallow saltwater environment are going to be susceptible to corrosion. However, what did come as a surprise was the fact that the steel platform from *Britannic* displayed an annual corrosion rate for the unprotected steel coupons almost three times faster than on *Titanic*.

This faster corrosion rate on *Britannic* may be a reflection of the greater and more diverse forms of life attaching to the steels at the much shallower depths, although the unknown factors are how much protection is being afforded to the paint coatings and the fact that the steels were not stressed during the sinking process (compared to *Titanic*). Yet, while the scientific study of *Britannic*'s wreck site is still at a relatively early stage, the initial results seem to suggest that although *Britannic* remains intact for the time being, one day the wreck may be subjected to a rather sudden collapse as the steel weakens to the point where it can no longer support its weight.

As with any shipwreck, we are living on borrowed time. It seems inevitable that one day *Britannic*'s structure will collapse and, although this should not come as any great surprise, without further scientific investigation there is no way of knowing how long that process might take.

Yet even at this late stage there may be a way forward. The UK Government is now actively supporting a long-term conservation project put forward by a consortium, including Governcheck Ltd, the British company which currently controls the government's title to the wreck. Hitherto, the practice has simply been to conduct a series of dives on the wreck in order to carry out an on-going mapping and visual documentation of the site, but in the event that diplomatic negotiations with the Greek Government are successful then, rather than being seen as *Titanic*'s forgotten sister, *Britannic* could soon become the central pillar in seeing all three Olympic-class liners in their true and full context.

The marker buoys for the floating deco station clearly indicate *Britannic*'s final resting place, barely 3 miles from the island of Kea. (Author)

In August 1995, Dr Robert Ballard also visited *Britannic*, utilising the US Navy's research submarine *NR-1*. Rated to a depth of 2,375ft, due to its nuclear reactor *NR-1* could have remained on the wreck indefinitely, the only limitation being the amount of on-board food supplies for the crew. *NR-1* was decommissioned on 21 November 2008, exactly ninety-two years to the day following the loss of *Britannic*. (Author)

A steel test platform was placed on *Britannic* in September 2003. After it was recovered in May 2009, the biofouling had completely encased the individual steel coupons. (Author)

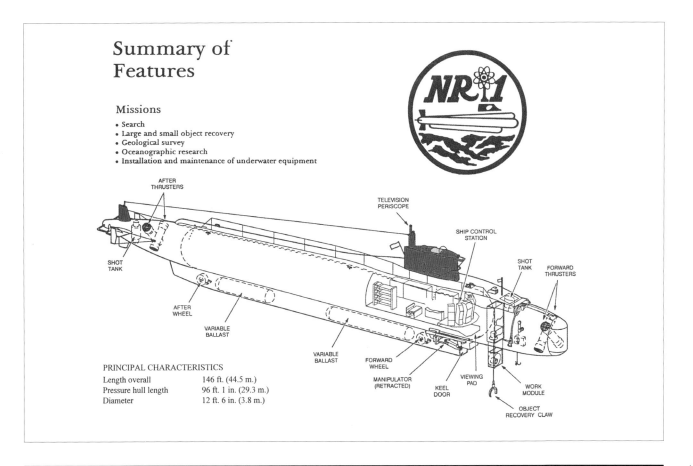

Summary of Features

Missions

- Search
- Large and small object recovery
- Geological survey
- Oceanographic research
- Installation and maintenance of underwater equipment

AFTER THRUSTERS

TELEVISION PERISCOPE

SHIP CONTROL STATION

SHOT TANK

SHOT TANK

FORWARD THRUSTERS

AFTER WHEEL

VARIABLE BALLAST

VARIABLE BALLAST

FORWARD WHEEL

MANIPULATOR (RETRACTED)

KEEL DOOR

VIEWING PAD

WORK MODULE

OBJECT RECOVERY CLAW

PRINCIPAL CHARACTERISTICS

Length overall	146 ft. (44.5 m.)
Pressure hull length	96 ft. 1 in. (29.3 m.)
Diameter	12 ft. 6 in. (3.8 m.)

Left: A composite sonar of the wreck made in 2003. (Bill Smith)

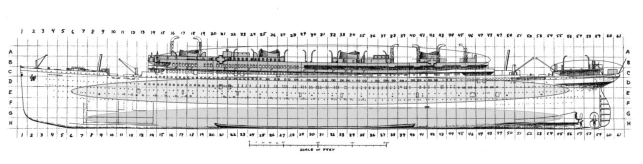

Left, below: Ken Marschall's 1995 diagram, originally designed for in-house use to assist in navigation around the wreck and updated to illustrate the concentration of life. At the topmost part of the wreck (red) are colonies of marine worms and sponges, while the upper edge of the wreck (blue) is dominated by a variety of sponges. Below this area (green) lies a flatter level of biofouling, made up of smaller sponges, hard and soft red coralline algae, with some apparent green algae and saddle oysters. The underside of the wreck is dominated by saddle oysters and other small fouling organisms. (Ken Marschall Collection)

Technical divers decompressing on a floating deco station. A forty-minute dive on *Britannic* requires a deco time of five hours so that the gas bubbles can be dissolved from the divers' bloodstream and body tissue. (Leigh Bishop)

Right: Aboard RV *Aegaeo* in 2008, with the Hellenic Centre for Marine Research (Elkethe). The technology included the two-man submersible *Thetis*, rated to 610m, and the MAX Rover ROV. (Author)

Four images of the wreck of
Titanic, taken in 2005, clearly
emphasising the differences
in the marine biofouling when
compared to the wreck of
Britannic. (Lone Wolf Media)

Britannic's port anchor, still in its hawse pipe. (Antonello Paone)

Top: A deck railing near to the breach beneath the forward well deck, now heavily encrusted with saddle oysters. (Antonello Paone)

Below: One of the four fallen bridge engine telegraphs, still hanging by its chains over 40ft above the seabed. (Antonello Paone)

Below: Another fallen engine telegraph, almost completely lost in the marine growth. (Kostas Katsaros/HCMR)

Left: The bridge steering wheel pedestal, now fallen from its mounting. This station was only used when the ship was being navigated in enclosed coastal waters. (Antonello Paone)

Above: A lonely anemone illustrates just how barren the seabed of the Kea Channel really is as you move away from the artificial oasis created by the wreck of Britannic. (Kostas Katsaros/HCMR)

Below: *Britannic*'s port running light would be a handsome trophy for any diver, but the combination of depth and the supervision of the Greek Marine Antiquities department means that *Britannic*'s wreck remains practically intact. (Leigh Bishop)

Two views of *Britannic*'s wheelhouse telemotor pedestal, almost completely hidden by the marine growth. (Antonello Paone & Kostas Katsaros/HCMR)

A diver swims past the port bridge wing house. Although the wreck seems almost completely intact, the thinner steel used in the bulwarks is long gone. (Leigh Bishop)

A diver swims above *Britannic*'s officers' quarters on the port-side boat deck. This area on *Titanic* is dominated by rusticles but on *Britannic* the sponges are more dominant. (Leigh Bishop)

Left: One of the fallen windows in the area of the bridge. (Kostas Katsaros/HCMR)

Below: The foremast still remains attached to the forecastle, but the top of the mast shows clear evidence of having been bent through over 90 degrees as it touched the seabed. (Kostas Katsaros/HCMR)

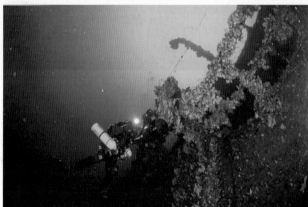

Above: A diver swims over the raised roof of the lounge. In the background one of the smaller Welin davits remains firmly attached to the boat deck. (Antonello Paone)

Right: A closer detail shot of the aft gantry davits on the port boat deck. The lifeboat tiers, davit pivot and worm gear are now completely frozen in place by the biofouling. (Dan Burton)

All of *Britannic*'s propellers remain above the seabed, although a fishing net dangling from the rudder means that the starboard propeller is less visible. (Antonello Paone)

Britannic's port propeller, which on 21 November 1916 was responsible for all of the casualties when the ship sank. (Antonello Paone)

Britannic's central propeller was cast in solid manganese bronze, with a diameter of 16ft 6in. (Kostas Katsaros/HCMR)

Below: The marine creatures have long since dispensed with *Britannic*'s pine decks, but the ghostly outlines of the wooden planks are highlighted by the ridges of caulking. (Kostas Katsaros/HCMR)

Examples of the sponges that have colonised the wreck. The plaque was laid on the wreck in 1997 in memory of Jacques Cousteau. (Kostas Katsaros/HCMR)

Some of the fallen lamps still safely in the lamp locker in the forward well deck. (Antonello Paone)

Right: An interesting comparison to Captain Smith's bathroom on the wreck of *Titanic*. Contrary to popular belief, this is not Captain Bartlett's bathroom, although it is located near to the bridge. The four taps provided hot and cold salt and fresh water. (Leigh Bishop)

Below: Inside the officers' quarters only a few floor tiles remain in situ, the loose fittings having fallen to the lower starboard side. (Antonello Paone)

Above: One of the most remarkable shots from inside *Britannic*, showing the spiral staircase in the fo'c'sle down which the firemen would descend when on their way to the boiler rooms. (Leigh Bishop)

Left: Among the fallen debris just aft of the bridge are tangles of electrical cables and possibly also evidence of what are believed to be the pneumatic tubes which took messages from the radio room to the bridge. This area in particular is earmarked for further investigation in the future. (Antonello Paone)

APPENDIX 1

THE OLYMPIC-CLASS LINERS

	Olympic	*Titanic*	*Britannic*
Registered No.:	131346	131428	137490
Port of Registry:	Liverpool	Liverpool	Liverpool
Year & No. of Registry:	1911 (39)	1912 (24)	1915 (93)
Gross Tons:	45,323.82	46,328.57	48,157.90
Net Tons:	20,894.20	21,831.34	24,592.24
Length (between perpendiculars):	852ft 6in	852ft 6in	852ft 6in
Beam:	92ft 6in	92ft 6in	94ft
Bulkheads:	15	15	16
Water Ballast Tanks:	17	17	17
Capacity (Tons):	5,726	5,726	5,843
Indicated Horsepower:	50,000	50,000	50,000
Nominal Horsepower:	6,906	6,906	7,150
Speed:	21 knots	21 knots	21 knots
Signal Letters:	HSRP	HVMP	JMDK
Registration Closed:	4 February 1939	31 May 1912	18 December 1916
Engines:	2x Inverted Direct-Acting Triple Expansion, 1x Low-Pressure Turbine		
Cylinders:	2 at 97in, 1 at 84in, 1 at 54in		
Length of Stroke:	75in		
Shafts:	3		
Boilers:	29 (24 double-ended and 5 single-ended)		
Furnaces:	159		

Construction Data

	Olympic	*Titanic*	*Britannic*
Harland & Wolff			
Yard No.:	400	401	433
Ordered:	31 July 1908	31 July 1908	23 October 1911
Keel Laid:	16 December 1908	22 March 1909	30 November 1911
Builder's Slip:	2	3	2
Framed to Height of			
Double Bottom:	10 March 1909	15 May 1909	12 March 1912
Fully Framed:	20 November 1909	6 April 1910	27 February 1913
Fully Plated:	15 April 1910	19 October 1910	20 September 1913
Launched:	20 October 1910	31 May 1911	26 February 1914
Delivered:	31 May 1911	2 April 1912	8 December 1915

APPENDIX 2

THE LOG OF HMHS *BRITANNIC*

First period of service

Depart	Arrive
Belfast: 11 December 1915	Liverpool: 12 December 1915
Liverpool: 23 December 1915 (0020hrs)	Naples: 28 December 1915
Naples: 29 December 1915 (1550hrs)	Mudros: 31 December 1915
Mudros: 3 January 1916 (1535hrs)	Southampton: 9 January 1916
Southampton: 20 January 1916 (1151hrs)	Naples: 25 January 1916 (0700hrs)
Naples: 4 February 1916 (1515hrs)	Southampton: 9 February 1916
Southampton: 20 March 1916 (1626hrs)	Naples: 25 March 1916
Naples: 27 March 1916 (1600hrs)	Augusta: 28 March 1916
Augusta: 30 March 1916 (1500hrs)	Southampton: 4 April 1916

Second period of service

Depart	Arrive
Southampton: 9 September 1916	Cowes: 9 September 1916
Cowes: 24 September 1916 (1740hrs)	Naples: 29 September 1916
Naples: 1 October 1916	Mudros: 3 October 1916
Mudros: 5 October 1916	Southampton: 11 October 1916
Southampton: 20 October 1916 (1630hrs)	Naples: 25 October 1916
Naples: 26 October 1916 (1642hrs)	Mudros: 28 October 1916 (0800hrs)
Mudros: 30 October 1916 (1205hrs)	Southampton: 6 November 1916
Southampton: 12 November 1916 (1423hrs)	Naples: 17 November 1916
Naples: 19 November 1916	

Sunk: 21 November 1916, Kea Channel, Aegean

APPENDIX 3

CAPTAIN CHARLES ALFRED BARTLETT

Name: Bartlett, Charles Alfred

Born: 21 August 1868 (London)

Educated: Cowper Street School, London

Apprenticed: D. Bruce Clippers, Dundee, and began career with the British India Company in 1888 before joining the White Star Line in 1894

Ordinary Certificate No.: 018359 (London, 1893)

Retired: 31 December 1931

Died: 15 February 1945 (Liverpool)

Ship	Reg No.	Appointed	Route	Rank
Jumna	93291	12 March 1891	Mediterranean	Second Mate
Dorunda	73759	26 April 1893	East Indies	Second Mate
Jelunga	98596	12 January 1894	East Indies	Second Mate
Doric	87847	15 June 1894	Australia	Second Mate
Gothic	102119	23 January 1897	Australia	Second Mate
Gothic	102119	17 March 1898	Australia	First Mate
Georgic	105326	29 March 1900	USA	Second Mate
Georgic	105326	1 January 1901	USA	First Mate
Teutonic	96334	20 February 1901	USA	First Mate
Celtic	113476	4 October 1901	USA	First Mate
Teutonic	96334	1 November 1901	USA	First Mate
Oceanic	110596	18 March 1902	USA	First Mate
Celtic	113476	11 May 1903	USA	First Mate
Armenian	105338	29 October 1903	USA	Captain
Germanic	70932	22 April 1904	USA	Captain
Victorian	105334	6 December 1904	USA	Captain
Canopic	113408	19 April 1905	USA/Mediterranean	Captain
Gothic	102119	5 February 1906	Australia	Captain
Republic	118043	25 July 1906	USA	Captain
Cymric	106989	4 September 1906	USA	Captain
Romanic	109441	2 February 1907	USA/Mediterranean	Captain
Cedric	115354	3 April 1907	USA	Captain
Britannic	137490	14 December 1915	Hospital ship	Captain
Britannic	137490	4 September 1916	Hospital ship	Captain

1907	Royal Decoration (RNR retired)
1914	Captain RNR (22 June)
1916	Elected Younger Brother of the Trinity House
1919	ADC to HM (until 1921)
1920	CBE (Civil Division) for Services during the War
1921	Member of RNR Advisory Committee; 14 October made commodore on RNR Retired List
1931	Mariner Warden of the Honourable Company of Master Mariners

APPENDIX 4

CASUALTIES OF THE SINKING OF HMHS *BRITANNIC*

Nine Officers and Men of the Royal Army Medical Corps

Lieutenant John Cropper (posthumously promoted captain) (age 51)

12423 Sergeant William Sharpe (age 39)*

33642 Private Arthur Binks**

81292 Private George James Bostock (age 23)

52640 Private Henry Freebury (age 31)

84010 Private Thomas Jones

41692 Private George William King (age 24)

40213 Private Leonard Smith

35188 Private William Stone (age 23)

Twenty-one men of the Mercantile Marine

Robert Charles Babey (trimmer, age 24)

Joseph Brown (fireman, age 40)**

Thomas Archibald Crawford (fourth butcher, age 27)

Arthur Dennis (trimmer, age 20)

Frank Joseph Earley (fireman, age 47)

Charles Claude Seymour Garland (steward, age 35)

Leonard George (scullion, age 17)

Pownall Gillespie (second electrician, age 30)

George William Godwin (fireman, age 29)

George D. Honeycott (lookout, age 30)**

Walter Jenkins (second baker, age 39)

Thomas McDonald (assistant cook, age 24) (served as T. Taylor)

John George McFeat (fireman, age 29)

Charles James David Phillips (trimmer, age 24)**

George Bradbury Philps (fireman, age 41)

James Patrick Rice (steward, age 23)

George Sherin (greaser, age 35)

William Smith (fireman, age 29)

Henry James Toogood (steward, age 48)

Thomas Francis Tully (steward, age 38)

Percival William Ernest White (trimmer, age 19)

* Buried in St Trias churchyard, Kea, on 21 November 1916; body moved to the New British Cemetery on the Greek island of Syra, Cyclades, in 1921.

** Buried on 22 November 1916 in what is now the Naval and Consular Cemetery, Drapetsona, Piraeus.

The names of the seven missing RAMC servicemen are commemorated on the Mikra Memorial at Thessaloniki, Greece. The names of the missing eighteen crewmen are included on the Merchant Marine Memorial, at Tower Hill in London.

BIBLIOGRAPHY AND SOURCES

Books

Anderson, Roy, *White Star* (T. Stephenson & Sons, 1964)

Ballard, Dr, Robert, D., & Archbold, Rick, *Lost Liners* (Madison Press, 1998)

Beaumont, Dr John C.H., *The British Mercantile Marine During the War* (Gay & Hancock, 1919)

———, *Ships and People* (Geoffrey Bles, 1926)

Bellou, N., Smith, C., & Papathanassiou, E., *Britannic Shipwreck Survey – Report of Field Operations: 17th–22nd September 2008* (Hellenic Centre for Marine Research, 2008)

Chirnside, Mark, *Olympic, Titanic, Britannic: An Illustrated History of the Olympic Class Ships* (The History Press, 2012)

Cullimore, Roy, & Johnson, Lori, *Microbiological Evaluation of the Potential At-Site Corrosion of the Steels Used in the Construction of HMHS Britannic* (Droycon Bioconcepts Inc., 2009)

Fleming, Rev. John A., *The Last Voyage of His Majesty's Hospital Ship Britannic* (Wordsmith Publications, 1998)

Jessop, Violet, *Titanic Survivor* (Sheridan House, 1997)

Johnson, Lori, *Final Report of September 2003 Expedition – Scientific Examination of the HMHS Britannic* (Droycon Bioconcepts Inc., 2003)

Louden-Brown, Paul, *The White Star Line* (Titanic Historical Society Inc., 2001)

Mills, Simon, *HMHS Britannic: The Last Titan* (Shipping Books Press, 1992)

———, *Preliminary Findings of Expedition to the Wreck of HMHS Britannic, Kea Channel* (Governcheck Ltd, 2000)

———, *Hostage to Fortune: The Dramatic Story of the Last Olympian, HMHS Britannic* (Wordsmith Publications, 2002)

———, *HMHS Britannic 2003 Expedition Report: Kea Channel, 1st–12th September 2003* (Governcheck Ltd, 2005)

Moss, Michael, & Hume, John R., *Shipbuilders to the World: 125 Years of Harland & Wolff, Belfast 1861–1986* (The Blackstaff Press, 1986)

Mullins, C.R., *Report for Marine Forensics Panel: Coal Analysis of Sample 137490* (Minton, Treharne & Davies Ltd, 2000)

Oldham, Wilton J., *The Ismay Line* (The Journal of Commerce, 1961)

Plumridge, John H., *Hospital Ships and Ambulance Trains* (Seeley, Service & Co., 1975)

Thomas, Lowell, *Raiders of the Deep* (Heineman, 1929)

Other Sources

Engineering magazine (27 February 1914)

Hospital Ship *Britannic* website: http://hmhsbritannic.weebly.com

Public Record Office of Northern Ireland (PRONI)

Shipbuilder magazine (February 1914)

Titanic Commutator (Titanic Historical Society Inc.)

UK National Archives

Britannic Expeditions

1976	Jacques Cousteau
1995	Robert Ballard
1997	Kevin Gurr/IANTD
1998	Nick Hope/Starfish Enterprise
1999	Jarrod Jablonski/GUE
2003	Carl Spencer
2006	John Chatterton & Richie Kohler
2008	Hellenic Centre for Marine Research (Elkethe)
2009	National Geographic (expedition abandoned following the death of lead diver Carl Spencer)

Britannic Documentaries

The Cousteau Odyssey: Calypso's Search for the Britannic (The Cousteau Society for KCET, 1977)

Titanic's Lost Sister (Varied Directions for NOVA, 1996)

Doomed Sisters of the Titanic (MPH Entertainment for The History Channel, 1999)

Inside the Britannic (Brentwood Communications for Discovery Channel, 2002)

Titanic's Doomed Sister (Carlton International for National Geographic, 2004)

The Curse of the Titanic Sisters (Carlton International for Channel 5, 2004)

Britannic: Titanic's Doomed Sister (Lone Wolf Documentary Group for History Channel, 2007)

In the Shadow of the Titanic (BBC Newsline, 2008)

INDEX

THE TITANIC COLLECTION

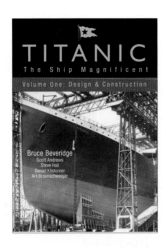

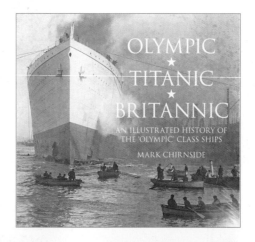

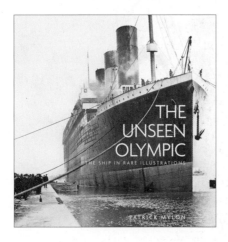

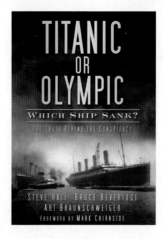

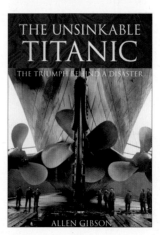

For the full Titanic experience visit The History Press website and follow the Titanic link

www.thehistorypress.co.uk

For stories and articles about Titanic, join us on Facebook